A BOOK BY ALEXANDER O THORNE

RISING ABOVE THE
E-MYTH

WHAT EVERY SUCCESSFUL ENTREPRENEURS KNOWS

UNDERSTANDING PROBLEMS IN SMALL BUSINESSES AND FINDING SOLUTIONS

RISING ABOVE THE E- MYTH

UNDER-STANDING PROBLEMS IN SMALL BUSINESSES AND FINDING SOLUTIONS

ALEXANDER O THORN

Copyright © 2023 by Victor Austine

All rights reserved. No part of this publication may be reproduced, distributed, or transmitted in any form or by any means, including photocopying, recording, or other electronic or mechanical methods, without the prior written permission of the publisher, except in the case of brief quotations embodied in critical reviews and certain other noncommercial uses permitted by copyright law. For permission requests, addressed "Attention: Permissions Coordinator," write to the publisher, addressed at the address below.

vaustine5@gmail.com

Table of content

INTRODUCTION

Why This Book Is Important

CHAPTER 1

THE EVOLVING SMALL BUSINESS LANDSCAPE

CHAPTER 2

BEYOND THE E-MYT

CHAPTER 3

PUTTING A STRONG BUSINESS FOUNDATION IN PLACE

CHAPTER 4

FINANCIAL INTELLIGENCE FOR ENTREPRENEURS

CHAPTER 5

BUILDING A WINING TEAM

CHAPTER 6

SYSTEMS AND PROCESS STREAMLINING

CHAPTER 7

ENGAGING CUSTOMERS IN THE DIGITAL ERA

CHAPTER 8

THE ENTREPRENEUR'S PERSONAL DEVELOPMENT PATH

CHAPTER 9

FUTURE-PROOFING YOUR ENTERPRISE

CONCLUSION

INTRODUCTION

Why This Book Is Important

The environment of the modern corporate world is continually changing. The media is full with start-up unicorn stories and rags-to-riches success stories, making entrepreneurship more alluring than ever. This setting inspires a large number of people to start their own businesses, frequently motivated by enthusiasm, creative ideas, and the prospect of financial freedom. Underneath this shining veneer, however, is a far more complicated reality that is sometimes tainted by unanticipated difficulties, errors, and misconceptions. This highlights the significance and importance of **"Rising Above the E-Myth: Understanding Problems in Small Businesses and Finding Solutions."**

- Displacing Pernicious Myths

[1]This book's primary goal is to dispel the "E-Myth," a widely held belief that the only requirements for success as an entrepreneur are enthusiasm and a good concept. The truth is far more complicated, as many discover all too late. While important, passion is just one element. Many enthusiastic company owners have been misled by the lack of a comprehensive grasp of business, including finance, operations, and human resources. This book acts as a lighthouse, dispelling these myths and providing a more accurate, realistic image of owning a company.

- Closing Information Gaps

Understanding the many dimensions of operating a company and having topic knowledge are two very different things. Even if an artist may produce works of art, does she also know how to sell them, handle funds, or interact with clients? Recognizing these gaps in knowledge, "Rising Above the E-Myth" works to close them. It offers a thorough overview, covering topics that company owners could neglect or be ignorant of, ensuring them have a complete understanding of managing a firm.

- Prevention-Based Problem-Solving

Entrepreneurs in all industries and geographical areas encounter a number of common difficulties. One may avoid typical hazards by proactively addressing these difficulties by

---

[1]

anticipating them and comprehending them beforehand. This book not only discusses these issues but also provides tried-and-true tactics, best practices, and ideas that may help organizations succeed—even during difficult times.

- A Resilience Road map

Volatility, uncertainty, complexity, and ambiguity define the corporate environment. Resilience becomes crucial in such a setting. This book provides entrepreneurs with the mentality, resources, and tactics needed to create companies that are not only successful but also resilient and adaptive to shifting market conditions via its in-depth material.

To sum up, "Rising Above the E-Myth" is more than simply a book—it's a necessary tool for any business owner. This book provides vital insights that will help you sail the entrepreneurial waters with confidence and competence, regardless of where you are in the idealization process, dealing with the difficulties of an established firm, or anywhere in between. Its core competency is its capacity to develop passionate company owners into knowledgeable, strategic, and adaptable business leaders. This book stands out as a beacon of clarity in a world full of noise and endless diversions, making it an essential tool in the business arsenal.

Deeper Exploration of the Entrepreneurial Myth

The Entrepreneurial Myth, often known as the E-Myth, is fundamentally a persuasive myth that promotes the belief that entrepreneurial success is mostly determined by enthusiasm and a fresh idea. It implies that one can overcome all challenges and ensure commercial success by just following their passion. This idealized idea has a certain charm since it conjures up pictures of driven people turning their ideas into successful businesses on their own.

But in practice, being an entrepreneur is far more complicated and subtle. While passion is a motivator, Unmasking the E-Myth shows that it accounts for just a portion of the equation. Understanding all facets of operating a company in its entirety is necessary for true success. These elements include successful marketing, operational efficiency, strategic planning, financial management, and the sometimes-disregarded skills of delegation and team management.

By dispelling this fallacy, we realize that becoming an entrepreneur involves more than just following your passion. It involves carefully balancing that enthusiasm with a sound business strategy. It's about realizing that there are many problems in the business world that can't be fixed by desire alone. This revealing casts doubt on the premise that anybody with a business idea can become prosperous overnight. Instead, it emphasizes how crucial it is to arm oneself with the information, abilities, and coping mechanisms needed to successfully traverse the challenging world of business.

Aspiring business people are given a wake-up call by Unmasking the Entrepreneurial Myth, which encourages them to consider their endeavors critically and comprehensively. It inspires individuals to embrace the gritty reality of company ownership rather than the idealized ideal. By encouraging people to approach entrepreneurship with a balanced mentality that recognizes the importance of both passion and business skills, a better understanding of the path is created.

Unmasking the E-Myth is essentially about escaping the constraints of simple narratives. It's about realizing that although enthusiasm may be the flame that starts the entrepreneurial flame, it can only be converted into a sustainable and successful company endeavor via strategic planning, ongoing learning, and a dedication to development. Through educated choices and a thorough approach to company leadership, entrepreneurs may survive in a world where the myth no longer exists.

A Deeper Exploration of the Need for Authentic Entrepreneurial

Education The entrepreneurial environment is both difficult and advantageous in an era of quick invention and widespread communication. Genuine entrepreneurship education serves as a compass for individuals hoping to navigate this turbulent sea of company endeavors successfully. However, why is it so crucial?

1. Relevance Beyond Traditional Learning - Theory vs. Practice: The corporate world is full of unanticipated situations,

despite the fact that many traditional courses teach theoretical information. By providing case studies, real-world examples, and simulations that prepare students for genuine business scenarios, authentic entrepreneurship education fills this gap.

- Cultivating Critical Thinking: This kind of education encourages students to ask the correct questions in order to develop their critical thinking and decision-making abilities rather of merely giving them the proper answers.

2. Mastery Over Change: - Future Forecasting: The capacity to anticipate changes in markets and industries is a crucial element of business success. Trend analysis is often included in authentic courses to assist students foresee and take advantage of new chances.

- "Adaptability Workshops": These classes educate company owners how to be flexible and change their plans as necessary to maintain and expand their enterprises.

3. Risk Management and Mitigation: In-depth Analysis: It's critical to comprehend prospective hazards. Entrepreneurs are given the means to overcome obstacles via courses that often involve SWOT analysis (Strengths, Weaknesses, Opportunities, and Threats) or comparable approaches.

- "Financial Prudence": Genuine entrepreneurial education focuses on financial management, assisting entrepreneurs in comprehending cash flows, investment plans, and risk diversification.

4. Developing an Entrepreneurial Mindset: *Building Resilience*: Failures and setbacks are inevitable in business. Through personal experiences and professional lectures, these courses foster resiliency in students and teach them the skill of rebounding.

- Workshops on Innovation: Innovation differentiates firms in a crowded market. These programs encourage creativity and encourage students to think creatively.

5. "Expanding Horizons through Networking" – "Mentor-ship Programs": Leveraging the experience of seasoned business-people may provide priceless insights. Authentic courses often include mentoring modules that connect students with professionals in the field.

- Collaborative Projects: These platforms may aid aspiring company owners in working together on projects, enabling them to pick up tips from colleagues, pool resources, and even identify possible partners.

In essence, the value of real entrepreneurial education goes beyond just acquiring information. It provides a support system, develops skills, and molds character. This education serves as the compass that directs entrepreneurs toward long-term success in a world where enterprises rise and fall with surprising frequency.

Of course! Let's deconstruct and clarify the idea behind "Charting the Course: From Common Mistakes to Business Mastery."

Explaining Charting the Course: From Common Errors to Business Mastery

Imagine setting off on a journey across unfamiliar territory. As a sailor needs a chart and compass to navigate the wide seas, so do ambitious company owners need direction to navigate the complicated business world. The navigation process in "Charting the Course: From Common Mistakes to Business Mastery" is comparable to that of the entrepreneur.

1. Identifying Common Errors: Any company initiative will inevitably make blunders when it first starts. These hazards, which include bad team relationships, poor financial planning, and misreading market demand, may sink even the most promising projects. The first step in the process is realizing these frequent errors. Understanding where others have erred can help you avoid making the same mistakes.
2. Learning and Adapting: Once business owners are aware of possible errors, the next step is to take what they've learned and move forward. This might include looking for a mentor, going to seminars, or just thinking back on the past.
    a. In order to better match the business model with market realities and needs, adaptation comprises adjusting strategies, making required pivots, and iterating the business model.

3. Developing a Stable Strategy: Entrepreneurs may create a better educated and solid company plan by learning from their prior errors. This entails establishing specific goals, figuring out who the target market is, and creating a strategy to get there.

- The road ahead is mapped out by strategy, which keeps organizations on track and away from possible pitfalls.

4. Implementation and Execution: A strategy is pointless without good implementation, no matter how well thought out it may be. Putting the strategy into practice, allocating resources, and advancing the company are all part of this phase. Being proactive, foreseeing difficulties, and having answers available are key.

5. Continuous Growth and Mastery: Business mastery is a journey rather than a destination. Entrepreneurs must embrace lifelong learning, keep current on industry developments, and continually hone their tactics.

- When a company not only survives, but flourishes, establishing itself as a leader in its industry, creating standards, and motivating others, that company has attained mastery.

The book "Charting the Course: From Common Mistakes to Business Mastery" summarizes the entrepreneurial journey from its early phases, which are rife with difficulties and mistakes, to a level of mastery when the firm becomes a beacon of success and excellence in its field.

CHAPTER 1

THE EVOLVING SMALL BUSINESS LANDSCAPE

The Situation of Small Businesses is Changing Small firms are not unaffected by the world's fast technical breakthroughs, changing customer preferences, and altering global dynamics. The small company environment today is constantly changing and evolving to take these changes into account. With insights into the current and future of small enterprises, this thorough investigation tries to unravel the numerous aspects of these transformations.

1. Historical Background

Understanding our past is necessary before we can comprehend the present situation. Small companies have always been regional operations that rely heavily on storefronts and word-of-mouth advertising. In the past, the small business scene was dominated by archetypes like bakeries, neighborhood tailors, and family-run grocery stores. Their activities were often family-focused, they had a small audience, and they used conventional techniques.

2. The Industrial Revolution

Due to the development of the internet and related platforms like Shopify, Etsy, and Amazon, businesses may now operate from their bedrooms and reach a global clientele. Fast forward to the 21st century, and the digital age has redefined what constitutes a "small business."

> **E-commerce Boom:** The ease of online buying and the abundance of options have helped e-commerce grow into a powerful force. Small companies may now function without a physical presence, significantly lowering expense and expanding reach.
>
> **Digital Marketing:** The days of limited advertising to local newspapers or radio ads are long gone. Even a small business may target certain demographics using platforms like Facebook, Instagram, and Google Ads, assuring a greater return on marketing investment.

3. Consumer Behaviors Changing

Consumers of today are quite different from those of the past. Their expectations and behavior have changed as a result of their access to knowledge and technological empowerment.

> **Demand for Personalization:** Modern customers want experiences that are tailored to them. They are more inclined to purchase goods or services from companies that cater to their tastes.
>
> **Value-driven Purchases:** Today's consumers are more selective about their purchases. They tend to support companies that share their beliefs, whether those values include community participation, ethical sourcing, or sustainability.

4. The Influence of the Gig Economy

Uber, Airbnb, and TaskRabbit are just a few of the platforms that have changed how small companies are defined. Nowadays, anybody can start their own business with only a smartphone.

- **Flexibility:** The gig economy gives entrepreneurs unparalleled freedom to choose their work schedules, services, and prices.

- **Diverse Opportunities:** The gig economy encompasses a wide range of industries, from ride-sharing to freelance writing, creating openings for a variety of skills and abilities.

5. The Double-Edged Sword of Globalization

For small firms, globalization has opened them new opportunities. International shipping businesses and platforms like Alibaba have made it simple to get goods from across the world. However, more competitiveness results from this interconnection.

6. Regulatory Obstacles

Regulatory organizations throughout the globe struggle to develop frameworks that assure justice, protect consumers, and do not inhibit innovation as the small company sector expands.

   Data Protection: To safeguard consumer privacy, laws like the GDPR in Europe have been put in place as a result of firms gathering enormous quantities of user data.

Fair Competition: Governments are becoming more watchful to prevent large digital companies from eclipsing or unfairly competing with small enterprises.

7. The Development of Niche Markets

The growth of specialty enterprises is one noticeable trend in the shifting environment. Specificity becomes advantageous when the market grows saturated. Specialized companies that serve a certain market or demand are making a name for themselves.

8. Adaptability in the Face of Adversity

Recent occurrences, like the COVID-19 epidemic, have put tiny enterprises throughout the globe to the test. Many changed, revised their company plans, or looked towards new income sources. This flexibility highlights how the terrain is always changing.

9. More Than a Buzzword: Sustainability

Small companies nowadays are incorporating sustainability into their operations more and more as a result of customer demand and sincere concern for the environment.

10. Uncharted Territory is the Future

The future is filled with limitless possibilities thanks to developments in AI, VR, and other technologies. Small firms will need to continue to be adaptable, knowledgeable, and innovative.

Conclusion On This Heading

The environment of small businesses is always changing, and it is a tapestry of chances, tribulations, and successes. The world of business will continue to be shaped, redefined, and revitalized by entrepreneurs despite the fact that change is a constant.

The Importance of Small Businesses

Small companies act as the subtle threads connecting communities, economies, and cultures in the vast tapestry of global trade. While enormous firms often take up much of the news, it is tiny enterprises that keep a steady pulse below the surface, performing important but sometimes underestimated functions. The many and crucial functions that small enterprises play in our society are examined in depth in this investigation.

1. Introduction

The phrase "small business" can immediately bring up ideas of neighborhood cafés, independent bookshops, or family-run farms. However, their influence goes well beyond the area around them. They are hubs for employment, innovation, and community cohesiveness.

2. Contributions to the economy

- **Job Creation:** The Small Business Administration (SBA) claims that traditionally, small firms have been primarily in charge of generating new employment. They provide varied workers possibilities, such as those for part-time work, seasonal employment, and flexible tasks.

Small enterprises make considerable contributions to a nation's gross domestic product (GDP). They promote economic expansion by creating and providing a range of goods and services.

Local Economies Boost: Spending money at a neighborhood small company increases the likelihood that it will be invested back into the neighborhood, stimulating the local economy.

3. Innovation Incubators

Small enterprises often set the pace for innovation, despite the fact that they may not have the financial weight of bigger organizations. They are better able to adapt, iterate, and develop since there are less administrative roadblocks and a stronger relationship to their clients.

Rapid Response to Market Needs: Small firms are better able to adapt their product lines in response to customer input and market needs than their bigger counterparts.

Less Red Tape: Small firms tend to be more efficient, which results in fewer levels of permission, encouraging a culture where new ideas are supported and implemented quickly.

4. Impact on the community and society

- **Creating Community Connections:** Tight-knit communities are often fostered by small enterprises. Owners promote neighborhood projects, know their clients by name, and fund regional events.
- **Cultural Preservation:** Many small enterprises, such as regional artists or authentic restaurants, contribute to conserving a community's cultural heritage by ensuring that customs, crafts, and regional cuisine continue to flourish in the face of globalization.

5. Increasing Customer Choice

Customers have a wide variety of options because to the variety of small enterprises. These businesses increase the market's diversity by offering consumers a choice of foods, apparel brands, and handcrafted goods.

6. Personalized Client Care

Small firms have a significant advantage in that they may provide individualized services. Better customer service, customized experiences, and a better understanding of client demands are often results of the relationship between company owners and their consumers.

7. Promoting the spirit of entrepreneurship

Small companies provide motivation. Aspiring business people often use local success stories as inspiration because they think that if one person can do it, so can they. Communities are encouraged to innovate and be ambitious by this cycle.

8. Adapting to Contemporary Trends

Many small companies have successfully switched to the internet in the digital age, using websites like Etsy, Instagram, or Shopify to increase their worldwide reach. Their capacity for adaptation demonstrates their tenacity and will to survive in a dynamic environment.

9. Sustainability and moral behavior

Small firms are increasingly promoting ecological and ethical practices, frequently motivated by links to the community and stronger relationships to their supplier chains. These companies often serve as role models for ethical business practices, from eco-friendly packaging to fair-trade sourcing.

10. The Road Ahead: Opportunities and Challenges

Small firms encounter difficulties, from legislative barriers to severe rivalry from bigger organizations, despite the enormous contributions they make. The development of technology, shifting consumer tastes toward locally produced goods, and a drive for sustainability globally, however, have given small enterprises a number of possibilities to carve out niches and continue to play vital roles.

Conclusion

In essence, small enterprises are not only for-profit organizations. They are the driving force behind innovation, the backbone of communities, and the stewards of cultural and customary preservation. For sustainable and equitable development, it is essential to acknowledge, support, and celebrate the critical role that small enterprises play as economies and societies change.

Navigating contemporary challenges and opportunities

Small enterprises become unsung heroes in the turbulent world of global trade, creating a story of creativity, resiliency, and social influence. Small enterprises are the ones that weave the fabric of our economies and society, while corporate giants often take all the attention. This investigation delves into

the many roles that small firms play, illuminating how they deal with current issues while seizing new chances.

1. The Unseen Foundations of Economy and Society

In a world when multinationals rule the news and skyscrapers stand in for conglomerates, tiny enterprises emerge as understated but influential characters. They cover a wide range of industries, from small shops and family-run restaurants to cutting-edge startups that upend established marketplaces. Once viewed through the prism of their effect, the apparently unassuming coffee shop or the local bookshop reveal a riveting tale.

2. Economic Growth and Resilience

Small firms play a crucial role in economies all around the globe, and they often hold the key to long-term development and job creation.

- **Job Creation:** Small firms have traditionally been the main source of new jobs, according to the Small Business Administration (SBA). These enterprises' flexibility and ability to cater to each customer's specific demands enable them to provide a variety of job options.
- **Economic Stimulus:** Small companies have an effect on the economy that extends beyond jobs. They foster an ecosystem of linked commerce by sourcing goods and services from surrounding vendors, which boosts local economies.

3. Innovation in a Shifting Environment

The ability of tiny enterprises to innovate under the limits of limited resources is one of their most remarkable characteristics. In overcoming today's issues, this ingenuity is especially noticeable.

- **Rapid Adaptation:** Small firms are able to quickly change their strategy and product offerings in response to shifting market conditions. They can react quickly to

changing customer tastes and new trends because to their agility, which frees them from the bureaucratic red tape that often holds back bigger firms.
- **Local Resilience:** Small enterprises often have an amazing capacity to remain tuned in to regional needs. They use their in-depth knowledge of local requirements to provide creative solutions that bigger organizations would ignore.

4. Creating solid connections within the community

Small enterprises are fundamentally knit into the social fabric of their local communities. This relationship goes well beyond business dealings and touches on issues of support and cohesiveness within the community.

- **Fostering Local Ties:** Small company owners are often active members of the neighborhood itself. As a result of their familiarity, customers develop a feeling of trust and loyalty, which motivates them to support their local economy by shopping there.
- **Cultural Nourishment:** Small companies often carry the torch of cultural preservation, whether it be via handmade goods or traditional food. They operate as cultural archives, ensuring that traditional ways of doing things survive in the face of globalization.

5. Meeting a Range of Customer Needs

The appeal of small firms rests in their variety; they provide a wide range of specialized goods and services to meet the needs of niche markets.

- **Tailored Offerings:** Small firms have the freedom to adjust their product lines to meet the needs of certain customer segments. The contemporary customer, who increasingly seeks for personalized experiences, is drawn to this personalized approach.
- **Curating distinct Experiences:** Small companies thrive at creating experiences that stand out in a world flooded with mass-produced alternatives, whether it's a cozy bookshop with a hand-picked selection or a craft brewery with distinct tastes.

6. Changing the Entrepreneurial Environment

Small companies are aspirational platforms for aspiring entrepreneurs as well as economic entities.

- **Inspiration and Motivation:** Success tales from the local area encourage and excite aspiring business owners. Others who want to establish their own businesses might use the experience of a local coffee shop owner or the founder of a tech firm as a model.
- **Innovation Incubators:** New ideas usually start in small enterprises. Small company starters often incorporate cutting-edge concepts into their enterprises, advancing the business landscape.

7. Accepting the Digital Transformation

Small companies are using digital technologies to expand their reach, broaden their clientele, and simplify operations in an age when technology is king.

- **E-commerce Integration:** To cross regional barriers, small enterprises are increasingly using e-commerce platforms. An artist working from a distant town may now market their goods to customers across the world.
- **Digital Marketing Mastery:** Small firms may compete for customer attention through social media and internet advertising without having a large advertising budget. They have more ability to magnify their brand voice thanks to the digital democratization.

8. An Aspiration for Sustainability

Small firms are responding to the demands from contemporary customers for ethical and sustainable business operations.

- **Sustainable Sourcing:** A lot of small firms place a high priority on ethical sourcing to make sure their goods have the least possible adverse effects on the environment and nearby populations.
- **Community Engagement:** Local participation is often a part of sustainability initiatives. Small companies may work closely with their neighborhoods to promote environmentally friendly behaviors and support charitable causes.

9. Threats to the Future

Small firms are skilled at navigating obstacles, but they are not immune to the intricacies of the contemporary world.

- **Regulatory Obstacles:** Complicated laws that are sometimes biased in favor of bigger organizations are a challenge for small enterprises.
- **Market Saturation:** In industries with low entry barriers, market saturation may be a problem, necessitating constant innovation on the part of enterprises in order to differentiate themselves.

10. Possibilities in a Globalizing World

Opportunities might be found amid obstacles, and tiny enterprises are using them to expand.

- **E-commerce Expansion:** The internet provides access to international markets, allowing small enterprises to overcome geographic limitations and connect with a wide range of customers.
- **Niche Dominance:** Specialty goods and services are becoming more popular in the age of mass manufacturing. Specialized needs are catered to expertly by small firms.

11. Conclusion: Moving Past Commerce and Into Culture

Small companies, in conclusion, are more than the sum of their transactions. They act as cultural keepers, incubators, inventors, and connections. They manage the problems of today with tenacity and agility, and they grab chances to stimulate development and change. They serve as a reminder that the human element is at the core of trade, binding together communities and encouraging the spirit of entrepreneurship as they maneuver through this complex tapestry of responsibilities.

CHAPTER 2

BEYOND THE E-MYT

Managing the Reality of Small Businesses, The notion of the "E-Myth" in the context of entrepreneurship serves as a sharp reminder of the contrast between idealized goals and the sometimes grim reality of operating a small firm. To properly appreciate the difficulties, prospects, and complex nature of small company efforts, it is imperative to get over this fallacy. This investigation probes the depths of negotiating the challenging environment outside the E-Myth.

1. Opening: Exposing the E-Myth

The "Entrepreneurial Myth," sometimes known as the "E-Myth," spreads the idea that successful businesspeople are largely motivated by a strong enthusiasm for their industry. This myth asserts that success as an entrepreneur requires just industry knowledge. This one-sided view obscures the many layers that come with owning a small company.

2. The Truth About Complex Roles

- **"Entrepreneur, Manager, and Technician":** In his book "The E-Myth Revisited," Michael E. Gerber describes the responsibilities of the Entrepreneur, Manager, and Technician. Effective role balancing is essential for small company owners to succeed.

- **Wearing Multiple Hats:** The Manager assures operational effectiveness, the Technician performs the technical tasks, and the Entrepreneur creates great plans. Small company ownership is a juggling act that involves navigating these positions.

3. Getting Around Financial Reality

- **Profit vs. Passion:** While enthusiasm is a motivating factor, profitability is the cornerstone of a long-lasting company. To secure the viability of the business, entrepreneurs must struggle with budgeting, cash flow management, and financial forecasting.
- **Risk Management:** The E-Myth does not equip business owners for the risky aspect of operating a company. Contingency planning, insurance coverage, and knowledge of legal nuances are all necessary for risk mitigation.

4. Customers-First Mentality

- **consumer Relationship Management:** Beyond knowledge, it is crucial to comprehend consumer wants and provide unique experiences. Investments in customer relationship management, feedback channels, and individualized service are necessary for small firms.

Effective marketing is a purposeful undertaking, not merely a matter of passion. To reach their target audience, business owners must understand digital marketing, branding, and market segmentation.

5. Scaling Obstacles

    - **The Growth Dilemma:** The E-Myth fails to address the difficulties of scaling. Strategic planning, recruiting, and system development are necessary for growth in order to retain quality while extending operations.
    - **Operational Efficiency:** The difficulty of preserving operational efficiency arises with increase. Process streamlining, embracing technology, and promoting a continuous improvement culture are all requirements for entrepreneurs.

6. Emotional Fortitude

    - **Leadership Loneliness:** Being an entrepreneur may be lonely. The emotional cost of making decisions, disappointments, and the weight of responsibility must be managed by owners.
    - **Coping Strategies:** Entrepreneurs require emotional intelligence in addition to enthusiasm. To weather the storms, they must develop coping strategies, look for mentoring, and build support systems.

7. Moving from "I" to "We"

    - **Team Dynamics:** The E-Myth often depicts the visionary as a lone figure. However, productive teams are what create successful enterprises. Entrepreneurs need to strengthen their leadership abilities, encourage teamwork, and inspire their employees.

- **Delegation and Empowerment:** It takes delegation to go from being a hands-on technician to an effective leader. Giving responsibilities to others empowers workers and frees business owners to concentrate on strategic issues.

8. The Continuous Learning Path

- **Adapting to Change:** The E-Myth downplays the significance of ongoing education. Entrepreneurs need to keep up with changing consumer trends, technical developments, and market trends.
- **Investing in Education:** Self-education is more important than passion. Entrepreneurs may manage altering environments with the help of courses, seminars, and industry events.

9. Embracing Growth and Failure

Failure as a stepping stone is not discussed in The E-Myth. Entrepreneurs must see failure as a teaching opportunity, learning from errors to spur expansion.

- **Iterative Approach:** Iterative efforts pave the way to success. Entrepreneurs need to learn from both their triumphs and mistakes in order to adapt, improve, and pivot.

10. Finale: From Myth to Reality

In essence, recognizing the multifaceted nature of entrepreneurship is the process of getting beyond the E-Myth. It's about realizing that although passion is the flame, strategic planning, business savvy, customer centricity, and teamwork light the path. A route that defies myth and emerges as a tribute to their commitment and resiliency is carved out by small company entrepreneurs as they traverse a maze of responsibilities, difficulties, and possibilities.

Dissecting the Entrepreneurship Myths

The world of entrepreneurship is often shrouded in a glittering aura, offering an array of unbounded potential, ground-breaking discoveries, and inspiring success stories. However, entrepreneurship is rife with myths, falsehoods, and half-truths, just like any other field. It is crucial to analyze and dispel these fallacies in order to successfully navigate the tricky business seas. In order to distinguish reality from fiction, this investigation will look deeply into several commonly held assumptions regarding entrepreneurship.

1. The Allure of Entrepreneurship, introduction

When you hear the word "entrepreneur," you probably picture youthful tech moguls, prosperous businesses, and ground-breaking inventions. The truth is, however, more complex, varied, and sometimes less gleaming than it first seems. Numerous unreported anecdotes show the difficulties, setbacks, and complexity of the entrepreneurial road for every success story.

2. Myth 1: Entrepreneurs aren't created; they're born.

One of the most persistent fallacies is the idea that becoming an entrepreneur involves a certain set of abilities and character qualities that people are born with.

- **Reality:** Entrepreneurship may be fostered, even if certain personality qualities may be advantageous. People may learn entrepreneurial skills with the correct instruction, guidance, and experiences. With commitment and direction, anybody may start this path, regardless of their background.

3. Myth No. 2: You Need a Radical Idea

Many people are discouraged from starting their own businesses because they think that only revolutionary ideas can be successful businesses.

- **Reality:** Though creative ideas are important, putting them into practice is just as important—if not more so. Many successful firms are based on enhancing current concepts or serving specialized markets. Instead of a wholly original idea, it's often about the proper timing, market fit, and execution.

4. Myth 3: Entrepreneurs love to take risks.

Entrepreneurs are often portrayed as daredevils willing to risk everything on their business in popular culture.

- **Reality:** Successful business people often manage and reduce risks. Although they may be risk-tolerant, they are seldom careless. They recognize the significance of thorough market research, prepared decisions, and backup plans.

5. Myth 4: Success via entrepreneurship

Many people start their own businesses with the hope of making quick money and the attraction of profitable exits.

- **Reality:** Starting a company requires patience since many ventures take years to become profitable. There are many financial unknowns along the way, and not all business endeavors bring in enormous profit. Entrepreneurial financial success involves perseverance, patience, and wise money management.

6. Myth 5: Younger Entrepreneurs Have a Higher Chance of Success

Many people now assume that age is a limiting issue since the IT industry has promoted the idea of youthful entrepreneurs.

- **In actuality,** entrepreneurship has no age restrictions. Many thriving business people got their start in their 40s, 50s, or even later. Years of experience, networking, and knowledge may often be helpful in creating a successful company.

7. Myth 6: If You Build It, They Will Come

It is deceptive to think that a quality product or service would draw clients on its own.

Even the finest goods need excellent marketing, in reality. Any firm that wants to succeed must focus on developing a strong brand, understanding the demands of its clients, and creating an appealing value offer.

8. Myth 7: Businesspeople Must Work Alone

According to the "lone wolf" concept, business owners must be lone warriors who wage their own fights.

- **Reality:** The keys to entrepreneurship success include building a solid team, looking for guidance, and networking. Collaboration rather than solitude often results in more thorough methods and better decision-making.

9. Myth 8: Starting a business provides immediate work-life balance

The appeal of flexible schedules and a perfect work-life balance draws many people to entrepreneurship.

- **Reality:** Entrepreneurship might need long hours, particularly in the beginning. Maintaining a healthy work-life balance demands conscious effort, time management, and boundary-setting.

10. Myth 9: Failure spells doom

Entrepreneurial stories often demonize failure and portray it as a fatal setback.

- **Reality:** The business route includes failure. The majority of thriving business people have encountered setbacks and used them as teaching opportunities to strengthen their tactics.

11. Myth 10: Business owners know all the solutions

It's a common fallacy that successful business owners always know what to do and how to solve problems.

- **Reality:** Entrepreneurs often travel new territory, making choices based on information at hand, instinct, and counsel. They are lifelong learners who are always searching out information and ideas.

12. Embracing the Authentic Journey is the conclusion.

When falsehoods are dispelled, entrepreneurship is still an exhilarating and rewarding path. It's full with obstacles, doubts, and defeats, but it's also teeming with chances for development and success. Aspiring business owners will go out on this path with realistic expectations, readiness, and a sincere love for their endeavor if they understand and dispel common falsehoods.

Identifying the Route to Real Business Success

Like any worthwhile undertaking, building a successful business involves a number of twists, peaks, valleys, and sometimes roundabouts. We must break down the factors that contribute to business success, dispel the misconceptions that surround it, and provide a practical road map if we are to really understand how hard it is to be successful in business. This investigation aims to provide a thorough manual for comprehending the components of real commercial accomplishment.

1. Decoding Business Success Introduction

The phrase "business success" is sometimes obscured by media coverage of unicorn businesses or stories of instant successes. In truth, these success stories are really about commitment, strategy, iteration, and adaptation. We must first explore the genuine meaning of success before we can set out on our path.

2. Developing a Vision

The vision of a company acts as its compass. It offers focus, meaning, and a base upon which all methods may be constructed.

- Developing a Vision Statement: This goes beyond just forecasting future sales or market share. It involves comprehending the company's raison d'être, or main goal.

- Vision as a Motivator: A compelling vision acts as an inherent motivator, steering teams through difficult situations and fostering clarity in decision-making.

3. Having Specific Goals

Objectives provide checkpoints on the path to success while the vision provides guidance.

- **The Power of SMART Goals:** Goals ought to be Time-bound, Specific, Measurable, Achievable, and Relevant. This structure guarantees responsibility, clarity, and viability.
- **Aligning Goals with Vision:** To ensure that plans and activities are coordinated, objectives should always be in line with the business's overall vision.

4. Putting Together a Cohesive Team

The most important resource for a business is not its cash, technology, or even its product—it is its staff.

The importance of cultural fit and alignment with the company's values cannot be overstated when it comes to hiring.

- **Investing in Team Development:** Growth opportunities, mentoring, and ongoing learning promote team cohesiveness and performance.

5. Customer-Centrality

Power dynamics have changed in the digital era to favor consumers. Their opinions, tastes, and loyalty may make or ruin a company.

- **Understanding the Customer:** This includes data analytic s, market research, and surveys. It is crucial to

have a thorough awareness of the wants, problems, and preferences of the consumer.
- **Iterating Based on input:** In the era of social media and rapid reviews, modifying goods or services in response to client input is not just a good idea—it's necessary for survival.

6. Embracing Innovation and Technology

Modern companies cannot afford to fall behind technologically.

- **Digital Transformation:** It is essential to use technology to improve customer experience, simplify processes, and optimize the supply of goods and services.
- **Fostering an Innovation Culture:** Teams that are encouraged to create, experiment, and perhaps even fail, come up with ground-breaking ideas.

7. Financial Intelligence

Although a crucial criterion, profitability is not the only one that identifies a successful firm.

- **Effective Budgeting:** This entails estimating income, planning for spending, and wisely allocating resources.
- **Understanding Cash Flow:** A company may seem to be prosperous on paper but yet have liquidity problems. Effective cash flow management is crucial for maintaining operational viability.

8. Creating a Robust Supply Chain

In a globally integrated economy, supply chains may be affected by disturbances in one region of the globe.

- **Diversifying Suppliers:** Dependence on a single source too much might leave a company vulnerable. Supply chain disruption risks may be reduced through diversification.
- **Adopting a Just-in-Time Approach:** When properly implemented, this inventory management method may increase effectiveness and save costs.

9. Brand development and marketing

Brand identity may set a company apart from its rivals in a crowded market.

- **Creating a Brand Narrative:** Each brand has a unique history, and when skillfully told, this history may have a powerful emotional impact on consumers.
- **Leveraging Digital Marketing:** Online channels, including social media and search engines, provide unrivaled chances for interaction, brand growth, and targeted marketing.

10. Getting Used to Change

Change is the only constant in the corporate world. Landscapes may quickly change as a result of market forces, technological developments, and international events.

- **Staying Informed:** Business executives may stay informed by regularly updating their market research, going to industry conferences, and networking.

Building a Flexible Business Model: Businesses that can pivot, adapt, and re-strategize in response to shifting conditions are more likely to withstand storms and come out stronger.

11. Social responsibility and morality

Businesses nowadays are social actors in addition to being economic ones.

- **Ethical Decision Making:** Adhering to ethics may improve a brand's reputation and customer loyalty in many areas, from sourcing procedures to staff interactions.
- **Participating in Corporate Social Responsibility:** Supporting neighborhood projects, advancing sustainability, and implementing green practices may appeal to socially aware customers and advance larger societal objectives.

12. Finale: The Constant Journey

Success in business is more of a journey than a destination. Continuous learning and adaptation are key.

CHAPTER 3

PUTTING A STRONG BUSINESS FOUNDATION IN PLACE

The Guide to Long-Term Success. Every majestic monument, lofty skyscraper, and lasting construction stands tall and unwavering because of the strength of its foundation. Similar to this, in the world of business, an organization's longevity, resiliency, and success are often decided by the strength of its underlying components. This article seeks to help both prospective business owners and seasoned industry professionals comprehend the value of building a solid company foundation and the measures to do so.

1. Introduction: The Importance of Business Foundations

A company that is founded without a strong foundation is likely to experience instability, inefficiency, and even run the danger of failing early, just as a home constructed on sand is vulnerable to collapsing. A solid foundation gives the endeavor direction, clarity, and structure so it can face obstacles and seize opportunities.

2. The Aligning North Star

Any company's vision is the cornerstone of its foundation. This acts as the business's ultimate objective and the pinnacle of its objectives.

- **Creating a Clear Vision Statement:** This statement should capture the company's long-term goals and its core purpose. For all those involved, it gives them a feeling of direction and purpose.

3. Mission: The Plan for Achieving the Vision

The mission is the means to achieve the vision, which is the final goal. It offers practical guidelines and tactics.

- **Defining the Mission:** The mission statement should clearly outline the organization's main goals, key tactics, and strategy for realizing its vision.

4. Core Values: The Foundations of Integrity

Every choice, course of action, and plan should be in line with the company's underlying principles.

- **Establishing and Upholding Values:** The company's culture, brand identity, and decision-making processes are shaped by its values, which may include a devotion to innovation, sustainability, or customer centricity.

5. Strategic Planning: The Roadmap,

A well-organized business plan acts as the blueprint for the company, including its objectives, plans, probable problems, and remedies.

Market research, financial predictions, operational plans, and marketing strategies are all part of comprehensive business planning. A well written company strategy attracts prospective investors in addition to directing internal operations.

6. Financial Stability: The Foundation

Even the most promising company ideas might fail if there is poor financial management.

- **Budgeting and Forecasting:** By foreseeing costs, estimating revenues, and wisely allocating resources, the company can continue to operate profitably.
- **Cash Flow Management:** Maintaining and controlling the cash flow makes sure the company can pay its debts and make investments to expand.

7. Developing Competent Teams: The Human Foundation

Any firm depends on its employees to survive. The key to success is selecting the appropriate team and supporting their development.

- **Recruitment and Training:** It is essential to draw in bright people, provide them the training they need, and make sure they share the vision and values of the organization.
- **Promoting a Positive Work Culture:** Productivity, creativity, and growth are all fueled by a motivated, engaged, and content staff.

The Safety Nets: Legal and Compliance Structures

The firm is protected from possible dangers by knowing and abiding by relevant rules and legislation.

- **Legal Incorporation**: Deciding on the best kind of business entity (sole proprietorship, partnership, or corporation) in light of the requirements and objectives of the enterprise.
- **Staying Updated:** The company is shielded from legal entanglements by routinely evaluating and complying to industry rules, tax laws, and compliance standards.

9. Customer Focus: The Vital Signs

Customers are the reason a firm survives and prospers. It is crucial to have a solid customer-centric basis.

- **Understanding the Target Audience:** Extensive consumer personas, feedback channels, and market research aid in customizing goods and services to suit client requirements.
- **Building Strong Relationships:** Setting client happiness as a top priority, taking complaints seriously, and appreciating feedback are the cornerstones of long-term success.

Conclusion: A Continuous Fortification Process

Building a solid company foundation requires ongoing evaluation, improvement, and fortification rather than being a one-time activity. Returning to and strengthening the foundation when the company environment changes, difficulties appear, and opportunities present themselves guarantees stability, resiliency, and long-term success. The real key to long-term success for entrepreneurs and business leaders is understanding the elements of this foundation and continually investing in its reinforcement.

The Science and Art of Vision and Mission Creation

The formulation of a company's vision and purpose stands out as a crucial exercise in the complex dance of business formation and growth. It combines the grace of art, which calls for inspiration and desire, with the accuracy of science, which necessitates clarity and concrete actions. This investigation clarifies the approach used to develop appealing vision and mission statements as well as the careful balance of the two components.

1. The Symphony of Vision and Mission: Introduction

Every renowned symphony has a maestro who directs the music, every masterpiece artwork begins with a clear vision, and the vision and goal of every prosperous company serve as the cornerstones of that enterprise. These components influence teams, direct choices, and explain goals to stakeholders.

2. Vision: The Dream Canvas

The company's ultimate goal and intended future state are depicted in the vision statement.

- **Artistic Element:** Imagination is necessary for a vision. It's about having huge dreams, letting your imagination run wild, and seeing your ultimate accomplishment.
- **Scientific Precision:** Although the concept may be idealistic, it must nevertheless be understandable to all parties involved. It should be a precise forecast of where the business wishes to go rather than a general or nebulous ambition.

3. The Action Blueprint for the Mission

The mission is the road map that shows how the organization intends to get there, while the vision is the final goal.

- **Artistic Element:** Constructing a mission entails creating a story. It narrates the company's strategy, practices, and ethos for realizing its goal.
- **Scientific Precision:** Concrete measures must be taken for the mission. In order to make sure that the high vision is more than simply a lofty statement, it is broken down into concrete goals.

4. Tapping into Stakeholder Aspirations via Emotional Resonance

Statements of the vision and purpose must emotionally connect with all stakeholders, including consumers, workers, and investors.

- **Artistic Element:** This entails being aware of the psyche, hopes, and wishes of people. The mission and

vision statements need to enthuse, stimulate, and engender pride.
- **Scientific Precision:** Ongoing feedback loops, surveys, and engagement activities may determine how effectively the vision and purpose connect with various stakeholder groups, enabling incremental improvement.

5.Integrating core values, item

The tenets and ideas that drive a company's operations are known as its core values. They need to be fully included into the mission and vision.

Values often come from the founders' own convictions, the culture of the business, and the legacy they want to leave behind.

- **Scientific Precision:** These numbers need to have practical applications. Not only must they be stated, but they must also be reflected in every activity, policy, and choice made by the firm.

6. Adapting to Change: Flexibility

Business is a dynamic field. Although fundamental, vision and purpose statements shouldn't be strict.

- **Artistic Element:** This calls for the capacity to dream fresh dreams, reimagine new worlds, and adjust to changing environments without losing the integrity of the original idea.

Regular evaluations, SWOT assessments (Strengths, Weaknesses, Opportunities, Threats), and market research all aid in adjusting the vision and mission to the reality of the present.

7 Making Statements: Useful Steps,

1. Gather varied teams for innovative brainstorming sessions. To go deep, use strategies like thought mapping or the "5 Whys."

2. **Competitor Analysis:** Recognize the market environment. Find opportunities and gaps.

3. **Feedback Loops:** Prior to making a decision, get input from a variety of stakeholders. Refine as necessary.

4. **Putting the Vision and Mission into Practice**

No matter how well constructed, a vision and goal are useless if they are just statements.

- **Artistic Element:** In order for these remarks to become tales that are often shared, applauded, and debated, leaders must take on these forms.
- **Scientific Precision:** Include the purpose and vision in operational guidelines, business regulations, and KPIs (Key Performance Indicators). When there are deviations, measure alignment and take remedial measures.

The Continuous Dance of Refinement (8. Conclusion)

Writing vision and mission statements is a process that combines art and science. It calls for imagination, forethought, accuracy, and analysis. Revisiting and updating these statements over time as companies expand and sectors change ensures that they stay true, directing the firm in the direction of its intended success. The vision and purpose act as the coordinated steps in the great dance of business, directing each action and choice in the direction of a standing ovation.

Strategic Blueprint: Forward-looking Business Planning

A painstakingly detailed map—a strategic plan that not only depicts the present situation but also anticipates the future—is necessary for navigating the complicated environment in the enormous world of business. The pillars that support a company's trajectory—business planning and forward-thinking—ensure that it is rooted in the present and well-prepared for the future. This investigation delves deeply into these ideas, clarifying their significance and the process that led to their integration.

1. Introduction: The Vitality of Business Strategy

The term "strategy" has its origins in the military jargon of the classical Greeks. Businesses need strategies to accomplish objectives, overcome obstacles, and take advantage of opportunities, just as a general requires a strategy to conquer territory. This strategic endeavor's core values include corporate planning and futuristic thinking.

2. Business Planning: The Present Situation

A business plan is a detailed document that outlines the firm's objectives, the justification for these objectives, and the strategies the company will use to attain these objectives.

- **Comprehensive picture:** A business plan's main objective is to provide a comprehensive picture of the company's operations, including information on its goods and services, market analysis, organizational structure, marketing and sales plans, and projected financial results.

Consider a business plan as the skeleton foundation for your organization. It serves as the framework on which a company is formed, providing it stability, direction, and shape.

3. Looking Ahead: The Horizon Beyond

A business strategy describes the immediate and immediate future, while forward-thinking focuses on seeing long-term trends, difficulties, and possibilities.

- **Visionary Outlook:** It entails stepping beyond of the familiar and the current to consider potential futures.
- **Preparation and Anticipation:** A company that is forward-looking will be proactive rather than merely reactive. It involves foreseeing change and being ready to shift course or adapt.

4. Coordination of forward-looking planning

A solid strategic blueprint is produced by fusing the short-term specifics of a company plan with the long-term vision of forward-thinking.

- **Short-Term and Long-Term Meet:** While the company plan may concentrate on short-term goals, including forward-thinking ensures that these goals are in line with long-term aims.
- **Agility Among Structure:** A strategic plan ensures that the firm is agile and able to adapt to new conditions while yet providing structure.
5. Important Parts of a Strategic Blueprint

1. **Executive Summary:** A description of the company's goals, values, and vision.

2. **Market Analysis:** A thorough investigation of market trends, market segments, rivalry, and potential growth areas.

3. **Organization and Management:** Detailed team profiles, responsibilities, and organizational structure.

4. **Service or Product Line:** Information on the goods or services, including their features, methods of manufacture, and issues relating to intellectual property.

5. **Customer acquisition and retention strategies in marketing and sales.**

6. **Financial Projections, including budgets, predictions, and financial plans.**

7. Forward-Thinking Insights: Prognoses on the development of the sector, prospective calamities, and long-term prospects.

Instruments and Methods

- **SWOT Analysis:** To help you make choices, identify your strengths, weaknesses, opportunities, and threats.
- **Pestel Analysis:** Examining Political, Economic, Social, Technological, Environmental, and Legal aspects of the company that might have an influence.
- **Scenario Planning:** Creating hypothetical future situations and preparing possible reactions.

6. Adopting Technology

Utilizing technology is essential for corporate planning and forward-thinking in the current digital world.

- **Data Analytics:** Using data to uncover patterns, spot trends, and arrive at well-informed judgments.
- **Digital Tools:** Software for forecasting, project management, and budgeting promotes accuracy and efficiency.

7. Constant review and revision

A strategic plan is a living document. Both the strategy and the business environment should change over time.

- **Regular Check-ins:** Quarterly or yearly reviews to evaluate the status of the project, any obstacles, and any potential possibilities.

- **input Mechanisms:** Obtaining input from stakeholders, including staff, clients, and customers, to improve strategy.

8. The Roadmap to Success

A strategic blueprint acts as the road map for the complex trip that is business, directing each choice, move, and endeavor. Businesses can handle difficulties, grasp opportunities, and steer themselves towards real, long-lasting success by carefully preparing for the now and intelligently forecasting the future. The strategic plan serves as the choreography for the dynamic dance that is the corporate world, ensuring that each step is deliberate, exact, and helpful in moving the project ahead.

CHAPTER 4

FINANCIAL INTELLIGENCE FOR ENTREPRENEURS

The capacity to comprehend and use financial data to make wise business choices is the core of financial acumen. Particularly for business owners, having sound financial judgment is not only advantageous but also essential. Entrepreneurship is not only about enthusiasm and creativity; it's also about making sure your business will be profitable.

What is financial acumen, exactly?

The abilities, information, and perceptions needed to make wise financial judgments are referred to as financial acumen. Understanding financial figures, planning ahead, and recognizing the financial effects of company decisions are all important.

Why Is It Important for Business Owners?

1. **Risk Management:** Business owners often have to make choices that carry varied degrees of financial risk. Financial savvy enables them to weigh these risks carefully.
2. **Business Sustainability:** Business owners must make sure their endeavor is lucrative in order for it to endure. This requires a thorough understanding of revenues, expenses, and profit margins.

3. **Stakeholder Trust:** Businesses are trusted by partners, workers, and investors. Building and sustaining this trust requires smart financial management.
4. **Strategic Planning:** Financial insights are essential to strategic business planning, assisting company owners in setting reasonable objectives and effectively allocating resources.

Important Elements of Financial Intelligence for Entrepreneurs:

1. **Understanding Financial Statements:** It's crucial to understand the fundamentals of cash flow statements, income statements, and balance sheets. These records provide a quick overview of the company's financial situation.
2. **Budgeting and Forecasting:** Business owners must be able to establish spending limits and anticipate future cash flow requirements. Forecasting entails foreseeing sales, expenses, and the financial effects of different company situations.
3. **Cash Flow Management:** Even firms that seem to be prosperous on paper can collapse as a result of cash flow problems. Entrepreneurs must keep an eye on and manage their cash flow to make sure they can pay their immediate obligations.
4. **Understanding Financing:** Entrepreneurs should be aware of the terms, charges (such as interest rates),

and possible repercussions of their financial actions before taking out a loan, looking for venture capital, or exploring other financing alternatives.
5. **Taxation and Compliance:** In order to stay out of trouble and avoid fines, business owners need have a basic awareness of their tax responsibilities, possible deductions, and required compliance.
6. **Return on Investment (ROI):** Entrepreneurs should think about the possible return when deciding whether to launch new projects or make investments. This guarantees that funds are directed to the places with the greatest effect.

Developing Financial Acuity:

Education: A lot of organizations provide courses in financial management for company executives who aren't in the finance industry. Additionally, accessible courses designed for businesses are offered on online platforms.

Financial Advisors To negotiate the complexity, it might be helpful to consult with financial specialists or accountants, especially in the early phases.

Networking: Talking to other company owners, becoming involved in organizations for professionals, or going to seminars may help you learn from first-hand experience.

Entrepreneurs may identify patterns, deal with problems, and reach educated choices by routinely evaluating financial accounts and analytics.

Recommendation:

For entrepreneurs, having strong financial judgment is essential. Understanding the financial environment and making wise judgments may be the difference between a venture's success and failure in the dynamic and sometimes unpredictable world of entrepreneurship. Entrepreneurs who take the effort to develop this skill set protect their companies and put them on a path for long-term success.

Breaking Down Financial Documents: An Entrepreneur's Complete Guide

Financial records are essential to the flow of information regarding a company's health, viability, and prospects in the world of business. These documentation may seem overwhelming to entrepreneurs, particularly those without a background in finance. But with the appropriate knowledge, they may develop into clear instruments that provide priceless insights. By dissecting these texts into their fundamental parts and explaining their relevance, this guide seeks to demystify them.

The Importance Of Financial Documents

Introduction Financial data is at the core of every company decision, whether it be one of growth, investment, or strategy modification. This information is condensed in financial statements, which provide a picture of the current state of the organization and potential future directions.

A snapshot of assets and liabilities is shown on the balance sheet (paragraph 2)

- **Understanding Assets:** An organization's assets are all of its possessions. They include:
- **Current Assets:** These are assets like inventories or accounts receivable that are anticipated to be turned into cash within a year.
- **Long-term Assets:** These might be tangibles like patents or intangibles like real estate or equipment.
- **Grasping Liabilities:** A company's liabilities are its debts. They include:
- **Current Liabilities:** Debts or commitments that are due within a year, including accounts payable or short-term loans.
- **Long-term Liabilities:** Debts such as mortgages or bonds that are due after one year.
- **Equity:** This is the remaining stake in the assets after obligations are subtracted. It is, to put it simply, what the owners really "own."

Understanding Earnings and Expenditures from the Income Statement (Profit & Loss Statement)

- **Revenue:** The top line, which represents the entire amount of money generated before any deductions for expenditures.
- **Cost of products Sold (COGS):** These are the direct expenses incurred by the firm while manufacturing products or services that are sold to customers.
- Gross Profit: The profit produced before subtracting operating expenses, calculated as Revenue minus COGS.
- **Operating expenditures:** These include expenditures for things like rent, wages, and advertising.
- **Net Income:** The final figure, which represents the profit after the deduction of all costs from revenue.

Cash Flow Statement: Monitoring Cash Movement

- **Operating Activities:** This part describes the revenue the firm generates from its main business activities. It consists of payments made to suppliers and staff as well as receipts from consumers.
- **Investing Activities:** Comprises money spent or earned through purchasing or disposing of assets, such as equipment or real estate.
- **Financing Activities:** This category includes cash flows from business dealings with owners and creditors, including stock issuance, dividend payments, and bank borrowing.

Understanding Owner's Equity Over Time: Statement of Changes in Equity.

- **Opening Equity:** The amount of equity at the start of the term.
- **Contributions & Withdrawals:** Funds added or taken out by the shareholders or owners.
- **Profits or Losses:** How the business's activities affect equity.
- **Closing Equity:** The equity balance indicating the company's net value at the conclusion of the term.

Notes to Financial Statements: Additional Information, paragraph six

This provides a thorough knowledge of the company's financial status by providing extra information or explanations concerning items on the main financial statements.

The value of routinely reviewing financial records

- **Informed Decision Making:** Entrepreneurs may make well-informed choices about anything from investments to operational adjustments thanks to accurate financial data.
- **Predicting Future patterns:** Historical financial data may provide insights into possible financial issues and future patterns.
- **Building Stakeholder Trust:** Regular, transparent financial reporting fosters relationships with all stakeholders, including workers and investors.
- Financial Documentation Tools & Software

The modern digital era provides a wide range of technologies, such as Quick Books, Xero, or Fresh Books, that automate and simplify the preparation and examination of financial information. These technologies eliminate human error while streamlining procedures.

Conclusion: Providing Financial Literacy to Entrepreneurs

When read and handled properly, financial papers are effective weapons in an entrepreneur's toolbox. They not only show how the company is doing right now, but they also determine where it will go in the future. Entrepreneurs can make sure they handle their company path with clarity, confidence, and accuracy by splitting these papers down and often revisiting them. Financial records serve as a compass to guide one toward success in the broad ocean of enterprise.

A Comprehensive Framework for Business Longevity: Designing a Sustainable Financial Strategy

A sustainable financial plan serves as a rock-solid anchor that keeps firms buoyant, robust, and moving in the direction of their goals amidst the ups and downs of the economic tides. Such a strategy aims to create a long-term financial plan that can weather storms and take advantage of good breezes, not only instant cash gains. This comprehensive manual covers the development and upkeep of a sustainable financial plan.

Introduction: The Financial Importance of Sustainability

Financial benefits made in the near term may be transient in an unstable global economy. Contrarily, sustainable financial methods put long-term stability first, ensuring that firms succeed across a range of economic climates.

Designing a sustainable financial strategy

The foundations of a sustainable financial strategy are listed in four section

Understanding Cash Flow: Businesses may sustain liquidity even during difficult times when they have a thorough understanding of cash inflows and outflows.

- **Debt Management:** This involves using debt wisely to fuel expansion while keeping levels under control.
- **Diversification:** By spreading out investments or income sources, a downturn in one sector won't devastate the company as a whole.
- **Conservative Financial Forecasting:** Being too cautious guarantees that you are ready for unforeseen financial difficulties.

1. Establishing a Robust Cash Reserve

A healthy cash reserve is one of the characteristics of a sustainable financial plan.

- **Importance:** Cash reserves may be used to cover operating expenses during a slump, ensuring that the company stays afloat.

- **Size of the Reserve:** Though this varies by industry, it is often advised to have 3-6 months' worth of operations expenditures on hand.

2. Slow Growth as opposed to Rapid Expansion

    - **Measured Steps**: Rapid development may be thrilling, but it also entails higher hazards. Sustainable business practices emphasize measured, steady development.
    - **Reinvestment:** Putting earnings back into the company for infrastructure, infrastructure growth, and research may pay off in the long run.

3. Caution in Risk Management

    - **Risk Assessment:** Consistently assessing possible financial risks, ranging from market declines to operational difficulties.
    - **Insurance:** Providing sufficient protection against unexpected occurrences, such as natural catastrophes and legal conflicts.

4. Effective Operational Expenditure.

    - **Operational Audit:** Periodic evaluation and simplification of activities to reduce inefficiency and increase efficiency.

- **Technology Integration:** Making use of contemporary technology may improve operations and, in the long run, save expenses.

5. Ethical financial management

Sustainability and ethics go hand in hand.

- **Transparency:** Honest, open financial reporting fosters stakeholder confidence and guarantees legal compliance.
- **Social Responsibility:** Ethical fundraising and investing decisions may provide results that are both financially and socially sustainable.

6. Stakeholder Communication and Engagement

Alignment with shareholders, creditors, workers, and other stakeholders is made possible via constant communication.

- **Regular Updates:** Regular financial updates promote confidence and make sure that all stakeholders are aware of the status and direction of the company.
- **Taking Feedback into Account:** Stakeholders often provide priceless ideas that may help mold a more sustainable financial plan.

7. Constant Learning and Adjustment

The financial environment is always changing. It's crucial to adjust and keep learning.

- **Staying Updated:** Attending financial workshops, seminars, and courses to remain current on market movements.
- **Benchmarking:** Analyzing the financial performance of the business in comparison to that of its competitors to find areas for improvement.

8. Assessing and Changing the Strategy

Even the most successful financial plans need to be reviewed from time to time.

- **Performance measures:** Using important financial measures to gauge how well the existing approach is working.
- **Iterative Refinement:** Adapting the strategy to the changing business environment based on assessments.

Collaborating with Financial Consultants: External Expertise

Although internal ideas are priceless, outside financial specialists may provide new viewpoints and specialized knowledge to develop a more sustainable plan.

9. Concluding Statement: The Path to Financial Sustainability

Developing a sustainable financial plan requires ongoing work rather than a single effort. It requires vision, flexibility, and a dedication to long-term stability above transient advantages. Such a plan makes sure a company stays a powerful force for future generations as well as in the present market. According to the proverb, "It's not about the destination, but the journey." When undertaken with caution and awareness, this road toward financial sustainability ends in long-term success.

CHAPTER 5

BUILDING A WINING TEAM

"Building a Winning Team: Using Talent for the Best Business Success."

The adage "teamwork makes the dream work" may seem overused, yet its core meaning holds true. Regardless of their size or sector, organizations are only as powerful as their teams. A strong, competent, and driven team may take a company to new heights, while a fractured team can make even the most promising of businesses fail. This investigation delves deeply into the science and art of building a successful team, a need for long-term commercial success.

Introduction:

1. The Strength of a Team

Every successful business is supported by a group of devoted people that work together. Their combined knowledge, wisdom, and viewpoints serve as the company's forward-moving force.

2. Vision Alignment: Purposeful Unity

It's essential to have a clear vision before you start assembling a team.

- **Shared Goals:** To ensure that everyone is rowing in the same direction, each team member should be aware of and committed to the organization's goals.

- **corporate Culture and Values:** Building a solid corporate culture based on distinct values guarantees that team members have guiding principles for their behavior.

3. Recruitment: The Basis of a Successful Team

The method used to choose team members is essential.

- **Skill Assessment:** In addition to assessing credentials, it's crucial to determine if a candidate's capabilities align with the requirements of the team.
- **Cultural Fit:** Ensure that prospective employees fit with the culture and values of the business.
- **Diversity and Inclusion:** An inclusive team fosters innovation and effective problem-solving by bringing a variety of viewpoints to the table.

4. Education and Training: Promoting Growth

A successful team must not just consist of the top candidates, but also be given the opportunity to improve over time.

- **Onboarding Programs:** The way new personnel are welcomed into the organization sets the tone for their tenure there.
- **Continuous Learning:** Ensuring team members continually upgrading their skills via seminars, courses, and training sessions.
- **Mentorship:** Associating less seasoned team members with seasoned experts helps hasten their integration and learning.

5. Team Dynamics' Lifeline Is Communication

The foundation of a cohesive team is clear and efficient communication.

- **Regular Check-ins:** Regular team meetings and one-on-one sessions aid in addressing issues, exchanging information, and coordinating goals.
- **Feedback Culture:** Promote a climate in which helpful criticism is freely expressed and accepted to support ongoing progress.

6. Motivation and Acknowledgement: Fueling Performance

Maintaining team motivation provides maximum output and dedication.

- **Intrinsic Motivation:** Match assignments to team members' interests and skills to ensure they really like their jobs.
- **Extrinsic Rewards:** Benefits, bonuses, and competitive pay all contribute significantly to motivation.
- **Recognition:** Regularly praising and honoring accomplishments, large or little, lifts spirits.

7. Flexibility and work-life balance

Offering flexibility may considerably increase team satisfaction in today's changing workplace.

- **Flexible Work Hours:** Giving team members some latitude in choosing their working hours may boost output and job happiness.
- **Remote Work:** With the help of modern technology, teams may work remotely, ensuring them strike a balance between their personal and professional obligations.

8. Teambuilding: Promoting Compatibility

Regular team-building activities may greatly improve the cohesiveness of your team.

- Plan excursions or outings for the team so that they may interact and connect away from the office.
- **Collaborative Projects:** Promote cross-functional team collaboration on projects to break down departmental silos.

9. Conflict Resolution: Overcoming Obstacles

Teams will always have conflicts, but good conflict resolution ensures that production is not hampered.

Encourage team members to publicly voice their complaints in order to make them feel heard.

- **Mediation:** Having a third party mediate may help resolve more serious disputes.

The Cultivation Process Is Still in Progress

Building a successful team requires continuing work rather than a one-time effort. The dynamics of the team will alter as markets shift, firms expand, and individual team members advance in their careers. Businesses can guarantee their teams stay cohesive, engaged, and ultimately successful by continuously investing in recruiting, training, incentive, and communication.

The Recruitment Formula:

Getting and Keeping the Best Talent for Your Organization Success in the ever-changing corporate world depends on more than simply the quality of the goods or services being offered; it also depends on the skills, dedication, and imagination of the staff working behind the scenes. Finding people who share the company's vision, beliefs, and culture is a key component of the recruiting process, which goes beyond just filling open positions. Additionally, long-term talent retention is a concern. The recruiting formula, a deliberate method for luring and keeping top personnel for organizational performance, is covered in detail in this extensive reference.

Introduction:

1. Talent as the Motivator

A company's employees are its greatest asset. The hiring process establishes the standard of personnel that will support the expansion and success of the business.

2. Building a Strong Employer Brand

A genuine employer brand conveys the organization's culture, values, purpose, and what it's like to work there.

- **Communicating via Channels:** Use social media, business websites, and sector events to promote the company's employer brand.

3. Development of Strategic Job Descriptions

- **Detailed Role Description:** Clearly state the obligations, demands, and potential for advancement in the position.

List the necessary and desirable credentials to make sure candidates are a suitable match for the position.

4. Getting around the Selection Process

- **Structured Interview Process:** Create a standard set of inquiries to properly assess applicants.
- **Assessment Tools:** Use tests of applicants' skills, personality evaluations, and other tools to learn more about their suitability.

5. Cultural Fit Evaluation

Determine if the applicant is compatible with the company's principles, culture, and working conditions.

- **Behavioral Interviewing:** Inquire about the candidate's past behaviors to see how they relate to the company's culture.

6. Transparent communication

- **Honesty in Expectations:** To avoid misconceptions, clearly define the position, corporate culture, and expectations.
- **Feedback Loop:** Keep applicants informed about the progress of their applications to preserve a good image, even if they aren't chosen.

7. Excellence in Onboarding

- **Structured Onboarding:** An efficient onboarding procedure aids new recruits in integrating into their positions with ease.
- **Buddy System:** Assemble new employees with seasoned team members to facilitate faster integration and provide advice.

8. Retention strategies are essential for long-term success

- **Professional Development**: Encouraging workers' engagement by providing chances for development, skill improvement, and career advancement.
- **Recognition and prizes:** Regularly thank staff for their efforts with both material and verbal prizes.
- **Work-Life Balance:** To avoid burnout and preserve workers' wellbeing, promote a good work-life balance.

9. Developing Effective Leadership

- **Leaders as Role Models:** Create leaders who inspire their employees and uphold the company's ideals.
- **Empowerment and Autonomy:** Give workers the freedom to decide for themselves, promoting a feeling of empowerment.

10. Diversity and inclusion

- **Diverse Hiring Pool:** To encourage innovation and creativity, recruit individuals from a range of backgrounds, cultures, and experiences.
- **Inclusive Environment:** Establish an environment where all opinions are respected and heard.

11. Data-Driven Decision Making

- **Analytics in Recruitment:** Use data to evaluate the efficacy of hiring practices and enable ongoing development.

Track turnover rates and collect customer feedback to spot patterns that may be changed.

Conclusion: The Recruitment Formula's Long-Term Effects

The recruiting formula is a deliberate method that determines an organization's future; it is not merely a checklist. A company's capacity to innovate, be productive, and ultimately be profitable is impacted by its ability to recruit and retain outstanding personnel. Businesses can create a virtuous cycle that attracts, retains, and develops the best talent, ensuring organizational excellence for years to come, by developing a compelling employer brand, carefully managing the selection process, fostering an inclusive environment, and supporting employees' growth.

The Key to Organizational Excellence

Fostering a Collaborative and Productive Environment The importance of a collaborative and productive atmosphere has gained prominence in today's fast-paced corporate climate. The day when solitary departments and lone heroes were sufficient is long gone. The success of contemporary enterprises rests on the synergy of teamwork and an atmosphere that fosters productivity. This in-depth investigation goes into detail on the challenges of creating such an atmosphere and the many advantages that result.

1. The Paradigm Shift Introduction

The modern era's buzzwords are innovation and adaptation, both of which are products of a collaborative and productive environment. Organizations achieve remarkable success thanks to the synthesis of many ideas, experiences, and abilities.

2. The Collaboration Framework

- **Shared Vision:** Before cooperation to flourish, there has to be an overarching goal that each team member can get behind.
- **Open Communication Channels:** Open communication dismantles barriers and silos and promotes mutual respect and understanding.
- **Cross-functional Teams:** Encourage teams from other departments to collaborate and use their specialized knowledge to achieve shared objectives.

3. Physical Space: Collaboration-Oriented Design

- **Open Floor Plans:** Moving away from closed-off cubicles and toward open areas promotes impromptu conversations and connections.

Whiteboards, projectors, and comfortable seats are provided in designated meeting rooms to encourage brainstorming sessions.

- **Casual Collaboration Areas:** Relaxed seating and lounge-like settings may encourage casual conversations and idea sharing.

4. Developing a Productive Mindset Goal Setting: Setting goals that are clearly stated gives individuals and teams more direction and a sense of purpose.

- **Continuous Feedback:** Ongoing check-ins and constructive criticism guarantee that everyone stays on task and in agreement.
- **Time Management Training:** Give staff members the skills and tools to efficiently manage their time.

5. Digital Instruments and Platforms

The digital revolution has made it possible to increase productivity and cooperation using a variety of technologies.

- **Collaborative Software:** Tools like Slack, Trello, or Microsoft Teams provide streamlined task management, project tracking, and communication.

- **Cloud-based Solutions:** Programs like Google Drive or Dropbox make it possible for people to work together in real time on papers and presentations.

6. Promoting a Trust-Based Culture

- **Empowerment:** Giving team members responsibility over decisions and duties encourages a feeling of ownership.
- **Transparency:** Being open about a company's goals, difficulties, and successes fosters inclusion and trust.

7. Promoting a healthy work-life balance

An employee who is exhausted cannot contribute well. As a result, encouraging work-life balance has a direct influence on productivity.

- **Flexible Work Hours:** Giving workers the freedom to change their work hours may boost productivity and wellbeing.
- **Remote Work Options:** In the connected world of today, giving employees the option of working remotely may increase morale and productivity.

8. Development and Training

- **Skill Enhancement:** Regular training sessions and classes make sure team members remain knowledgeable and prepared to work together successfully.

- **Team Building Activities:** Events outside of the workplace, such as retreats or seminars, may promote cooperation and teamwork.
• Acknowledging and Honoring Collaborative Efforts
- **Reward Systems**: Set up incentives or recognition programs for groups who work well together.
- **Showcase Success Stories:** To motivate others, share examples of effective teamwork inside the organization.
• Handling Conflicts In A Positive Way
- **Conflict Resolution Workshops**: Provide team members with resources to resolve conflicts amicably.
- **Open Mediation:** Provide impartial forums for mediation where disputes may be addressed and resolved.

Continuous Assessment and Improvement

Implement tools to collect feedback on the collaborative and productive atmosphere, indicating areas that might be improved.

- **Iterative Changes:** Consistently review and improve tactics in light of customer feedback and changing business requirements.

Conclusion: A Collaborative and Productive Environment Has Multiple Benefits

Every person plays a different instrument in the huge symphony that is a company. The real beauty, however, is when these instruments coordinate in perfect harmony. To create this harmony, foster a collaborative and productive workplace. It's a conscious, continual effort, but the rewards are numerous: improved creativity, higher staff morale, increased efficiency, and ultimately, unmatched organizational greatness. This environment serves as a compass for firms as they traverse the complex web of the contemporary marketplace, pointing them in the direction of long-term success.

CHAPTER 6

SYSTEMS AND PROCESS STREAMLINING

Opening the Door to Excellence and Efficiency Maintaining efficiency and competitiveness in a business environment that is always changing takes more than just passion and vision; it also calls for a solid structure of systems and procedures. The accuracy of these systems and procedures is crucial for the efficient orchestration of activities, the smooth flow of information, and the efficient use of resources. In-depth discussion of the relevance of simplifying operations via thoughtful systems and procedures is provided in this article, along with tips for a successful implementation.

1. Getting Started: The Foundation of Business Operations Any successful business has a maze of procedures hidden under the surface. When these procedures are well defined and simplified, operations run smoothly, mistakes are reduced, and the business's overall efficiency is increased.

2. Recognizing Systems and Procedures
   - **Systems**: These are integrated collections of parts or processes that work in concert to accomplish a certain goal. Systems in business might include hardware, software tools, or processes.

- **Processes:** These are groups of related tasks that work together to change resources (inputs) into outputs (products/services). They are the particular actions done inside the system to finish a certain activity in detail.

3. The Desirability of Streamlining

    - **Efficiency:** Simplified procedures eliminate duplication and guarantee that each step contributes to the success of the project.
    - **Consistency:** Businesses may ensure consistent product or service quality, regardless of volume or size, by using standardized procedures.
    - **Clarity:** Having clear procedures gives workers a road map, which cuts down on uncertainty and promotes good decision-making.

4. Evaluating current operations

It's crucial to comprehend the present operating picture before streamlining.

    - **Audits:** Perform regular audits to spot inefficiencies, bottlenecks, or antiquated procedures.
    - **Feedback:** Get opinions from staff members who are leading these procedures. Their practical knowledge is priceless.

5. Utilizing Technology

Numerous instruments are available thanks to modern technology that are made to improve different company activities.

- Automation Tools: Programs like Integromat and Zapier automate routine processes to free you time for more worthwhile pursuits.
- **Project Management Platforms:** Programs like Asana, Trello, or Monday.com facilitate assigning, tracking, and finishing tasks.
- **Data Analytics:** Make use of analytics technologies to learn more about customer behavior, process performance, and other topics.

6. Training and ongoing education

The team's expertise should change together with the systems and procedures.

- **Regular Workshops:** Ensure that staff members are familiar with any new procedures or resources.
- **Feedback Loops:** Inspire staff to provide comments on recently installed systems and procedures.

7. Documentation: The Streamlining Blueprint

- **Standard Operating Procedures (SOPs):** Exact written instructions on how certain procedures go, providing uniformity and clarity.
- **Regular Updates:** To ensure that everyone on the team has access to the most recent information, documentation

for processes should be regularly updated to reflect changes.

8. Flexibility in Adaptation

Although streamlining seeks uniformity, it's important to stay flexible.

- **Change Management:** Be ready to modify procedures in response to customer feedback, unanticipated difficulties, or shifting market conditions.
- **Iterative Improvement:** Think on simplifying as a journey rather than a one-time undertaking. The key phrase should be constant progress.

9. Measuring Results

After installation, evaluate the effects of the simplified systems and procedures on a regular basis.

- **Key Performance Indicators (KPIs):** Metrics like as turnaround time, mistake rates, or customer satisfaction may provide perceptions into the efficiency of processes.
- **Regular Reviews**: Conduct reviews to evaluate how well corporate goals and procedures are aligned.

10. In conclusion, systems and processes work together.

Systematically enforcing a predetermined pattern is not the goal of process and system optimization; rather, it aims to provide a smooth rhythm for business activities. Businesses can do more with less resources when systems and processes work together effectively, promoting development, consistency, and agility. Streamlined systems and procedures are the unsung maestros directing an outstanding performance in the big theater of corporate operations.

The essence of operational efficiency

Operational efficiency is more than simply a buzzword used in boardroom discussions or a goal to go towards. An organization's basic values affect how well it functions, how well it serves its clients, and how well it can expand and adapt in a constantly shifting business environment. This in-depth investigation of operational efficiency offers insights into its significance, the elements that make up its basis, and techniques to improve it for long-term corporate success.

1. Getting at the Roots of Operational Efficiency

In every business process, operational efficiency is related to the ratio of input to output. It involves getting the intended outcomes with the least amount of waste, effort, time, and money. It's the art of streamlining processes to efficiently give the most value.

2. Why Operational Effectiveness Is Important

- **Cost Reduction:** Costs are often lowered as a result of efficient operations, improving profit margins.
- **Enhanced Productivity:** Teams can do more in less time thanks to streamlined procedures.

- **Client Satisfaction:** Quicker response times, consistent product or service quality, and better all-around client experiences are the results of efficient operations.
- **Adaptability:** A company that runs smoothly can adjust to market shifts or unforeseen difficulties with more ease.

3. The Foundations of Operational Effectiveness

- **Streamlined Processes:** Remove unnecessary stages from a process and make sure each stage contributes value.
- **Technology Integration:** Making use of cutting-edge technology to streamline, improve, and keep track of company operations.
- **Employee Expertise:** Assuring that staff members are knowledgeable, well-trained, and supportive of the business' operating objectives
- **Continuous Improvement:** Consistently evaluating and improving processes for better results.

4. Identifying the Present Situation

Understanding the present operational status is essential before improving operational efficiency.

- **Operational Audits:** Perform exhaustive audits to spot waste, inefficiencies, and bottlenecks.
- **Feedback Mechanisms:** To gauge the effectiveness of present operations, collect opinions from stakeholders, consumers, and staff.

5. Acknowledging Technological Solutions

   - **Automation Tools:** Use software to automate routine work so that human resources may be used for more complicated jobs.
   - **Data Analytics:** Make use of analytics to learn more about consumer behavior, market trends, and operational performance.
   - **Collaborative Platforms:** To improve communication, cooperation, and project management, use tools like Slack or Microsoft Teams.

6. Education and Development of Skills

   - Hold workshops on a regular basis to introduce new tools, technologies, or procedure modifications.
   - Certification Programs: Encourage staff to enroll in classes that improve their job-related abilities.
   - Mentorship Initiatives Assemble teams of less-experienced workers and seasoned experts for mentoring and learning.

7. Key performance indicators (KPIs) and metrics

   - **Choosing the Correct Metrics:** Find KPIs that are relevant to your business operations. Metrics like processing times, mistake rates, and customer response times may be among them.

- **Regular Monitoring:** Use dashboards and reporting tools to monitor these metrics on a regular basis to make sure operations stay on course.

8. Supply Chain Management Reconsidered

The supply chain is often a crucial operational component for firms that are product-focused.

- **Supplier Relationships:** Establish solid bonds with suppliers to guarantee dependability and quality.

Implement methods to monitor inventory levels in order to ensure appropriate stock levels and save carrying costs.

9. Creating an Efficiency Culture

- **Leadership's Role:** Leaders should uphold the principles of effectiveness and ongoing development.

- **Employee Incentives:** Implement incentive programs for groups of people or teams who make substantial contributions to increasing operational effectiveness.

10. The Function of Iteration and Feedback

- **Feedback Loops:** Set up platforms for staff to voice concerns about operational issues or recommend fixes.
- **Iterative Improvements:** Operations should be seen as dynamic systems that undergo continuous improvement depending on user input and performance metrics.

11. Addressing Obstacles and Challenges

Every path to operational efficiency will have obstacles.

- **Proactive Problem Solving:** Identify possible obstacles and create proactive solutions rather than taking reactive action.
- **Collaborative Approach:** Promote an environment where problems are solved creatively by working together to tackle them.

12. Operational Excellence as the Foundation of Business Excellence

Operational effectiveness is a journey rather than a destination. Businesses advance because of this undercurrent, which makes sure they provide value while making the most of their resources. The need of operational efficiency becomes even more crucial as the corporate environment grows more complicated. It serves as a guiding light for enterprises, making sure they not only survive but also grow in a cutthroat environment. Businesses may ensure their position as market leaders, both now and in the future, by realizing how important it is and working tirelessly to improve it.

Harnessing modern tools and technology

The digital revolution may be navigated for better business performance by using modern tools and technologies.

The rapid development of tools and technology has fundamentally altered how organizations function, interact, and provide value. Every organization, from tiny startups to well-established conglomerates, is racing to adopt the newest technological developments to improve customer experience, simplify operations, and promote creativity. This thorough book examines the fundamentals of using contemporary tools and technology, exploring their wide-ranging effects and how firms may successfully use them for long-term success.

1. Introduction: The Business Landscape of Technology

In the digital age in which modern organizations operate, technology serves as both an enabler and a crucial differentiator. By using the most recent tools and technology, you may choose to lead your industry or fall behind.

2. The Range of Contemporary Tools and Technologies

- **Cloud computer:** Offers organizations scalable computer resources, assuring data accessibility and cutting expenses for IT.
- **Artificial Intelligence (AI) and Machine Learning:** These innovations help companies gain insights, automate processes, and improve user experiences.
- **Blockchain:** In addition to cryptocurrencies, blockchain provides decentralized, transparent, and secure solutions for a range of commercial applications.
- **Internet of Things (IoT):** As more and more devices are linked together, organizations are better able to collect

real-time data, improve their operations, and provide novel solutions.

3. Advantages of Adopting Modern Tech Solutions

   - **Operational Efficiency:** Streamlined processes are facilitated by automated workflows, real-time data analytics, and effective resource management.
   - **Enhanced Decision-Making:** Data-driven insights empower companies to take calculated risks and seize opportunities.
   - **Scalability:** Thanks to modern technology, organizations may expand without seeing a corresponding rise in expenses.

4. Digital Transformation's Function

   - **Defining Digital Transformation:** It entails transforming whole company models, cultures, and customer experiences around digital capabilities in addition to embracing technology.
   - **Strategic Approach:** A clear plan should direct digital transformation, taking into account present capabilities, intended results, and possible barriers.

5. Selecting the Appropriate Tools and Platforms

   - **requirements Assessment:** Businesses must evaluate their requirements, difficulties, and goals before incorporating a new tool.

- **Cost-Benefit Analysis**: Calculate a tool's or technology's prospective ROI vs its expenses to ensure lasting value.
- **Compatibility and Integration:** Ensure that new technologies integrate with current systems and procedures without causing any disruptions.

6. Development of Training and Skills for Modern Tech

- **Regular Workshops:** Inform staff members on the newest tools, ensuring that they are knowledgeable and comfortable using them.
- **Specialized Training:** Specialized training sessions or courses may be required for complicated technologies like AI or blockchain.

7. Ethical Considerations in Technology Harnessing

- **Data Privacy:** As data grows in importance as a commercial asset, its acquisition, storage, and use must be lawful and considerate of users' privacy.
- **Transparency:** Companies should be open and honest about how they utilize technology, particularly when it affects stakeholders or consumers.

8. Potential Obstacles and Challenges

- **Resistance to Change:** Staff members used to the old ways may be resistant to the new.
- **Security Concerns:** New technological solutions, particularly ones that depend on the internet, may have security flaws.

- **High Initial Costs:** Investing in advanced technology might be expensive at first.

9. Impact Assessment of Integrated Technologies

    - Define and track metrics that measure the effectiveness of the integrated tools and technologies (Key Performance Indicators, or KPIs).
    - **Feedback Mechanisms:** Regularly collect staff and consumer feedback to comprehend the influence in the actual world and places for development.

10. Using technology to prepare for the future

    - **Continuous Learning and Adaptation:** Businesses should keep current as technology develops, adjusting as necessary, and seizing new possibilities.
    - **Culture of Innovation:** Encourage staff to investigate and test out novel technical solutions.

11. Taking Advantage of Technological Advancements in Conclusion

Utilizing contemporary tools and technology is now essential for firms' survival and development; it is no longer a choice. Despite its intimidating appearance, the digital world is full with potential for those who are ready to explore it with an open mind, a well-defined plan, and a dedication to lifelong learning. Businesses may improve their operations, improve customer experiences, carve out a position for themselves in the global market, and be prepared to take on the possibilities and challenges of future by skillfully integrating these tools and technology.

CHAPTER 7

ENGAGING CUSTOMERS IN THE DIGITAL ERA

"Engaging Customers in the Digital Era Strategies for Building Meaningful Connections" examines customer engagement in a digital age. "Engaging Customers in the Digital Era: Strategies for Building Meaningful Connections" examines customer engagement in a digital age.

Businesses are contending for attention in the huge, linked expanse of the digital age, not simply for market share. Unparalleled possibilities exist in the digital environment to engage clients in creative ways. However, the sheer amount of online interactions and material also poses special difficulties. Businesses need to discover innovative methods to engage their consumers if they want to stand out. This thorough manual looks into the nuances of client involvement in the digital age, providing ideas and tactics for forging sincere bonds.

1. The Digital Engagement Paradigm

Engagement in the digital era is more about resonance than it is about simple visibility. In order to connect with clients, businesses must meet their needs, beliefs, and goals.

2. Recognizing the modern digital consumer

- **Global and Diverse:** The digital client is not limited by location. They have diverse histories, cultures, and life experiences.
- **Informed and Empowered:** Customers who have access to information are often well-informed and have high standards.
- **Seeking Authenticity:** Customers are seeking for businesses that align with their beliefs and provide true experiences, rather than just items or services.

Personalization: The New Standard

Data analytics may be used to comprehend client preferences, habits, and pain areas.

- **Tailored Experiences:** Based on specific user information, provide personalized content, product suggestions, or interactive experiences.

4. Engagement across all channels

- **Seamless Interactions:** Assure that consumers enjoy seamless interactions with your business whether they use a website, mobile app, social media platform, or even in-person.
- **Unified Communication:** Consistent message, offers, and brand identity should be available across all media.

5. Content Remains King

- **Value-Driven material:** Produce informational, amusing, or inspiring material that provides real value.
- **Interactive Content:** To actively engage people, utilize polls, interactive videos, quizzes, and other dynamic content types.

6. Making Use of Social Media Platforms

- **Diverse Platforms, Diverse Strategies:** Be aware of the distinctive features and user demographics of each platform, from Facebook and Instagram to TikTok and LinkedIn.
- **Engagement Over Promotion:** Rather than merely pushing promotional information on social media, encourage actual conversations.

7. Establishing Communities

- **Forums and Discussion Boards:** Establish areas where consumers may interact, communicate, and debate topics pertaining to your business or sector.
- **Loyalty Programs:** Promote repeat encounters and honor devoted clients with exclusive deals, materials, or experiences.

8. Participating Through Experiences

- **Virtual reality (VR) and augmented reality (AR):** Provide immersive experiences, such as interactive 3D product demonstrations and virtual try-ons for clothing.

- **Webinars and Live Streams**: Organize in-person gatherings where consumers may learn, engage, and form connections with your company.

9. Reaction time and feedback

- **Active Listening:** Follow client attitudes on social media, in reviews, and in feedback channels.
- **Quick Responses:** Provide rapid responses to questions, comments, or other feedback to demonstrate your dedication to client pleasure.
-

10. Changing with New Digital Trends

- **Stay Updated:** Consistently revise your digital interaction tactics in light of new platforms, tools, and user trends.
- Continuous Learning: Promote a culture in which teams continually experiment, learn from their findings, and make adjustments.

Conclusion: Establishing Sincere Digital Connections

In the digital age, engaging clients requires constant innovation, authenticity, and agility. It's important to comprehend how clients are navigating the constantly changing digital world. Businesses can create sincere connections that go beyond screens and bytes, establishing loyalty, trust, and long-lasting relationships, by putting consumers at the center of their digital initiatives.

Crafting a resonant brand identity

Making a Timeless Impression in Audiences' Minds: Creating a Resonant Brand Identity

What distinguishes one brand from the competition in the crowded market when innumerable businesses compete for consumers' attention? Not only a logo or a snappy slogan will do; a brand's deeper essence, consistent experience, and values must also be considered. These components are combined with a strong brand identity to create a story that sticks in the minds of the audience. The basis for long-lasting brand loyalty and awareness is laid forth in this thorough book, which delves deeply into the art and science of creating a compelling brand identity.

1. Introduction: Beyond Pictures and Words

A company's attitude, purpose, and distinctive value proposition are all encapsulated in its brand identity, which is its essence. It is the constant character a brand presents in every contact, impacting impressions and choices.

2. Brand Identity's Foundations

- **Core Values:** These are the principles that a brand is built around. They direct messages, choices, and activities.
- **Mission Statement:** This explains the goal and reason for the brand's existence.

- **Vision Statement**: It outlines the brand's long-term goals and the influence it aspires to have on society.

3. Visual Branding Components

    - **Logo:** A logo, which is more than simply a graphic and captures a company's spirit, is often the most identifiable feature of that brand.
    - **Color Palette:** Different hues have different psychological effects. A constant color scheme guarantees audience recognition and emotional resonance.
    - **Typography:** Written text's look and style are crucial in expressing a brand's identity and guaranteeing readability across media.

4. Developing a Brand Voice

    - **Tone and Style:** The brand's tone should represent its beliefs and connect with its target audience, whether it is formal, lighthearted, authoritative, or friendly.
    - **Consistency:** A consistent brand voice makes it possible to recognize the brand on many platforms and in various media.

5. Brand Narrative and Messaging

Every brand has a narrative to tell—a journey and a purpose for being. Stories enthrall viewers, humanize businesses, and increase their memorability.

- **Unique Value Proposition (UVP):** Clearly state how the brand differs from competitors by catering to the particular demands or aspirations of the target market.

6. User Experience as an Integral Aspect of Brand Identity

- **Digital Presence:** Websites, apps, and other digital platforms have to provide simple-to-use interfaces that represent the brand's dedication to customer happiness.
- **Physical Touchpoints:** The design of shops, the packaging of their goods, even their business cards, should all be consistent with their brand identity.

7. Continually Remaining Consistent Across Touchpoints

- **Brand Guidelines:** A document including instructions on how to utilize logos, colors, fonts, images, and other brand components provides consistency across channels.
- **Regular Audits:** Regularly examine and evaluate brand touchpoints to make sure they are consistent with the brand identity.

8. Changing Without Losing Your Essence

Like living things, brands also develop. Any development, however, must to be natural, preserving the essential qualities while making adjustments for changing conditions.

- **Rebranding:** Occasionally, a big change in brand identity may be required, but it should be handled carefully to maintain audience connection and engagement.

9. Getting Stakeholders Involved in Brand Identity

Employee onboarding: Workers serve as brand ambassadors. Genuine customer interactions depend on their grasp of and adherence to brand identity.

- **Community Building:** Encourage a feeling of ownership and belonging by including devoted clients, fans, or followers in brand-related choices or adjustments.

10. Measuring the Impact of Brand Identity

- **Brand remember:** Evaluate how quickly and precisely consumers can identify and remember the brand.
- **Brand Perception Surveys:** Obtain feedback to determine how the brand is seen in relation to the identity it seeks to convey.
- **Engagement indicators:** Examine online interactions, social media participation, and other indicators to determine how well the brand identity is being received.

Conclusion: A Resonant Brand Identity's Long-Lasting Echo

To create a memorable brand identity is similar to carving a sculpture. The process of identifying, honing, and expressing a brand's essence in its most basic form is painstaking. When done well, it's about connection rather than simply recognition. A strong brand identity goes beyond transactions to establish loyalty, promote trust, and generate supporters. It makes sure that the brand's voice is recognized, repeated, and appreciated in the clamor of the marketplace.

Trends and ta tics in digital marketing

Digital Marketing Trends and Strategies: Exploring the Changing Digital Landscape for Brand Excellence

Similar to shifting sands, the digital marketing environment is continually changing due to technological breakthroughs, fluctuating customer behavior, and emerging social platforms. The ground-breaking tactic of today can be yesterday's news tomorrow. For companies looking to retain relevance and engagement in this dynamic market, keeping up with the most recent trends and strategies is not only advantageous but also essential. The latest trends and strategies that are shaping the world of digital marketing are highlighted in this thorough investigation, providing company owners with knowledge on how to properly use them.

1. Introduction: The Metamorphosis of Digital Marketing Since its debut, digital marketing has changed how companies communicate with their customers. It's a sector that is always evolving, from the early days of email marketing to the modern era of AI-driven campaigns.
1. The Development of Video Content

- **Livestreaming:** Websites like Twitch and Facebook Live have made real-time involvement a potent marketing tool for businesses.
- **Short-Form Video:** Thanks to the rise of apps like TikTok, short, interesting video clips have become very popular.
- **Videos in virtual reality** and augmented reality These provide engaging experiences that turn listeners into active participants.

3. voice Search and Smart Assistants, respectively.

- **Voice Search Optimization:** With the rise of smart speakers, content optimization for voice search is no longer optional.
- **Conversational Marketing:** The use of chatbots and virtual assistants powered by AI to engage people in ongoing dialogues on websites and mobile applications.

4. Individualization and hyper-individualization

- **Data-Driven Customization:** Adapting marketing messages and offers to specific tastes based on data gathered.
- **Dynamic material:** The presentation of material on websites or applications depending on the activities, interactions, or sources of a user.

5. Machine learning and artificial intelligence

- **Predictive Analytics:** Making use of AI to make predictions about potential customer behavior based on historical data.
- **Programmatic Advertising:** Automating real-time ad placements while more accurately and strategically targeting users.

6. Evolution of Social Media

- **Ephemeral material:** Stories on Facebook, Instagram, and Snapchat provide momentary yet compelling material that grabs users' attention right away.
- **Niche Platforms:** In contrast to the dominance of behemoths like Facebook and Twitter, niche platforms like Clubhouse are carving out their own distinctive markets.
- **Collaborations with Influencers:** Joining forces with micro and macro influencers for sincere brand endorsements.

7. Refinement of content marketing

- **Interactive content:** such as polls, quizzes, and infographics that prolong user engagement.
- **Long-Form Content:** Detailed essays, whitepapers, and guides that boost SEO ranks and build brand authority.

8. Strategy for omnichannel marketing

- **Unified Experience:** Consistent user experience and brand message across several digital touchpoints.

- **Data Integration:** Combining data from many sources to create a comprehensive understanding of client journeys.

9. Sustainable marketing and ethical advertising

   - **Green Marketing:** Emphasizing eco-friendly activities, goods, or projects to appeal to customers who are concerned about the environment.
   - **Transparent Practices:** Disclosing openly information on product source, business ethics, and sustainability initiatives.

10. Ten. Improving Mobile Marketing

    - **Mobile Optimization:** Assuring that websites, advertisements, and content are prepared for viewing and interaction on mobile devices.
    - **App-Based Marketing**: Using push alerts, offers, and in-app advertisements to engage users.

11. Data Security and Privacy

    - **GDPR and Other Regulations:** Following data protection laws to maintain user confidence.
    - **Transparent Data rules:** Disclose data collection, use, and protection rules in a clear and understandable manner.

12. Changing SEO Methodologies

    - **Voice Search Optimization:** Modifying SEO tactics to accommodate an increase in voice-activated queries.

- **Visual Search:** Sites like Pinterest and Google Lens provide picture searches, which calls for a change in optimization strategies.

13. The Function of Webinars and Virtual Events

- **Engaging Distant Audiences:** Webinars and virtual events have become more important as remote work and digital connections grow.
- **Hybrid Events:** Bringing together real-world events with online elements to appeal to a wider audience.

Staying Flexible in the Digital Marketing Odyssey, Conclusion

Trends and approaches change, entwine, and at times vanish in the vast fabric of digital marketing. The fundamental idea—understanding and engaging the audience—does not alter. Brands can manage the changing digital currents by being knowledgeable, flexible, and customer-focused. This will ensure that their messages not only reach their target consumers but also resonate strongly, creating long-lasting relationships. These relationships, which are fostered by clever digital marketing methods, will determine a brand's success and longevity as we go through the digital era.

CHAPTER 8

THE ENTREPRENEUR'S PERSONAL DEVELOPMENT PATH

The Entrepreneur's Personal Development Path: Building the Mindset, Competencies, and Resilience for Entrepreneurial Excellence, Entering the world of entrepreneurship involves much more than just starting a company or announcing a new product. It's a journey that is really personal, filled with learning, discovering, obstacles, and change. As the driving force behind their businesses, entrepreneurs must engage in their own personal growth in order to guide them toward success. This thorough manual digs into the subtleties of the personal development path of the entrepreneur, providing insights into its essential elements and the transforming impact it may have on the person and their firm.

1. Entrepreneurship and Personal Development Introduction

Entrepreneurship is fundamentally a manifestation of a person's goals, principles, and drive. Growth on both the personal and professional levels affects and shapes the other.

2. Fostering the Correct Mentality

- **Growth Mindset:** Accepting difficulties, learning from mistakes, and seeing failures as chances for improvement.

- **Adaptability:** The capacity to adjust one's course when necessary.
- **Visionary Thinking:** Looking forward, imagining prospective futures, and establishing challenging yet doable objectives.

3. Developing emotional intelligence (EI) is step three.

- **Self-awareness:** Being conscious of one's feelings, traits, and triggers.
- **Empathy:** Sharing and comprehending others' emotions, essential for group dynamics and customer connections.
- **Emotion Regulation:** Controlling irrational feelings and urges and remaining composed in stressful situations.

4. Developing Grit and Resilience

- **Endurance:** The capacity to endure difficulties, setbacks, and protracted periods of uncertainty.
- **Recovery:** Creating plans for overcoming setbacks and avoiding protracted slumps in motivation or burnout.
- **Relentless Pursuit:** Tenaciously pursuing objectives despite repeated setbacks or challenges.

5. Skill development and lifelong learning

- **Continuous Education:** Keeping abreast with market changes, technology breakthroughs, and industry trends.
- **Soft Skills:** Improving interpersonal abilities such as leadership, negotiation, and communication.

- **Networking:** Establishing and maintaining connections with role models, peers, and subject matter experts.

6. Well-being and Health

- **Physical Health:** Consistent exercise, a healthy diet, and enough sleep to preserve vigor and concentration.
- **Mental Health:** Stress reduction, mindfulness exercises, and getting help from a professional when necessary.
- **Work-Life Integration:** Striking a balance between work obligations and personal obligations while making sure none is ignored.

7. Seeking Recommendations and Reflection

- **Mentorship:** Talking with knowledgeable people who can provide advice, insight, and constructive criticism.
- **Self-reflection:** Consistently evaluating one's objectives, plans, and pace of personal development.
- **responsive to Feedback**: Promoting open dialogue among team members and being responsive to criticism.

8. Setting personal boundaries is step eight.

- **Time Management:** Setting priorities, establishing limits, and allotting time for rest and personal development.
- **Avoiding Overcommitment:** Appreciating boundaries, mastering the art of saying "no," and maintaining an equitable allocation of time and resources.

9. Accepting Failure in Your Teaching Career

- **Analyzing Mistakes:** Examine mistakes to gain insights and lessons rather than dwelling on failures.
- **Creating a Safe Space:** Promoting a Culture in Where Mistakes Are Viewed As Growth Opportunities, Promoting Innovation and Risk-Taking.

The Endless Journey of Personal Development: Conclusion

Entrepreneurship is a journey that involves development, failures, learning, and evolution rather than a straight line. Entrepreneurs who engage in their personal growth not only improve their skills but also enrich their companies, promoting cultures of creativity, resiliency, and success. Despite the difficulties along the way, the entrepreneurial spirit is refined and defined by these difficulties, leading to satisfaction on both a personal and professional level.

Nourishing the Entrepreneurial Spirit

Entrepreneurship is a way of life, not just a vocation. It involves more than simply operating a company; it involves adopting a mentality that is fueled by creativity, resiliency, and the search for meaning. To navigate the chances and difficulties that come with the territory, the entrepreneurial spirit must be nurtured. This in-depth manual explores the subtleties of encouraging the entrepreneurial spirit and provides insights into its essential elements and how they contribute to both corporate success and personal joy.

1. Introduction: Unveiling the Entrepreneurial Spirit's Essence

People that have an entrepreneurial spirit are driven to take risks, invent new things, and rebel against the current quo. It serves as the motivation that keeps business owners moving forward in the face of difficulty.

2. Passion as the Foundation
   - **Authentic Enthusiasm:** Fostering a strong, sincere passion for the company concept or endeavor.
   - **Sustaining Energy:** Using passion as a motivator even in trying circumstances.
   - **Infectious Zeal:** Spreading the enthusiasm among the staff, the investors, and the clients to create a common goal.
3. Developing Creativity
   - **Embracing Exploration:** Promoting a culture that values experimentation, ideation, and creative problem-solving.
   - **Cross-Pollination:** Getting creative inspiration from diverse fields, sectors, and viewpoints.
   - **Iterative Innovation:** Adopting the idea of ongoing development and refining strategies, services, and products.
4. Purpose-Driven Initiatives
   - **Clarity of Purpose:** Identifying a purpose for the endeavor that goes beyond monetary benefit.

- **Social Impact:** Aligning the company's efforts with social issues that share the entrepreneur's beliefs and improving society.
- **Sustained Motivation:** To sustain a high level of motivation, link everyday struggles and tasks to the broader goal.

5. Accepting Risk and Building Resilience
- **Calculated Risk-Taking:** Juggling bold choices with in-depth investigation and analysis.
- **Learning from Setbacks:** Using mistakes as learning opportunities and incorporating what you've learned into your future tactics.
- **Building Resilience:** Strengthening one's mind and heart to withstand the ambiguities and volatility of entrepreneurship.

6. Thriving on Ambiguity

- **Adapting to Change:** Adopting a mentality that embraces change and adapts swiftly to changing conditions.
- **Uncertainty as Opportunity:** Seeing uncertainty not as a cause of pain but as a blank canvas for creativity and invention.
- **Flexible Mindset:** Accepting turning points, pursuing novel avenues, and grasping unanticipated chances.

7. A spirit of networking and cooperation

- **Building a Supportive Network:** Putting oneself in the company of mentors, peers, and advisers who may provide direction and insights.
- **Collective Wisdom:** Making use of the information and experiences that the entrepreneurial community has to offer collectively.
- **Collaborative Ventures:** Combining the resources and talents of like-minded businesses or organizations.

8. Continuous Learning and Growth

   The development of an inquisitive mind that strives to learn from experiences, difficulties, and failures.

   - **Adopting a Student Mindset:** Realizing that every circumstance presents an opportunity to grow and learn.

9. Juggling aspiration and wellbeing

   - **Healthy Ambition:** Aiming high while keeping equilibrium and preventing burnout.
   - **Work-Life Harmony:** Ensuring that personal priorities are given equal weight with professional pursuits.
   - **Mindfulness Practices:** Using techniques like mindfulness or meditation to improve self-awareness and lessen stress.

Legacy Building, 10.

   - **Long-Term Vision:** Thinking about how the project will affect not just the present but also future generations.

- **Empowering Others:** Giving team members and heirs the chance to continue the entrepreneurial spirit.

The Ever-Growing Flame of Entrepreneurial Spirit, Conclusion

Fostering an entrepreneurial spirit is similar to stoking a fire that already burns brightly inside of a person. It's about encouraging innovation, facing obstacles with a resilient and goal-driven mentality, and embracing enthusiasm. This attitude fosters not just professional success but also personal development, contentment, and the development of a lasting legacy that goes beyond financial gain. This particular mentality enables entrepreneurs to prosper, innovate, and make a lasting impression on their industry and the lives they touch in a world characterized by change and complexity.

Lifelong Learning and Work-Life Balance

Maintaining Growth During Activities Lifelong Learning and Work-Life Balance are Two crucial elements often dance together in the complex dance of entrepreneurship, the pursuit of knowledge and the search for a healthy balance between work and life. Achieving work-life balance and continuing education aren't simply side issues; they're essential cornerstones of success for both individuals and their businesses. This in-depth manual explores the nuances of lifelong learning and work-life harmony, providing insights into the interdependence of the two and how entrepreneurs may balance them for long-term success and joy.

1. Introduction: Learning and Balance Are Dual Imperatives

Entrepreneurship is more about lasting endurance than a quick dash. It takes a combination of ongoing education and a balanced attitude to work and life to navigate this route.

2. The Value of Lifelong Learning as a Mindset
   - **Continuous Adaptation:** Accepting the fact that markets, technology, and industries are always evolving.
   - **Curiosity as Fuel:** Developing an attitude that looks for lessons to be learned from experiences, difficulties, and failures.
   - **Skills Evolution**: Understanding that skills evolve and must be replaced by new ones.
3. The Multiple Dimensional Learning Spectrum
   - **Formal Education:** Pursuing diplomas, certificates, and courses to get a solid understanding of the subject.
   - **Self-Directed Learning:** Exploring niche interests via books, podcasts, online courses, and other resources.
   - **Industry Insights:** Participating in conferences, workshops, and seminars to keep abreast of emerging trends and advances.
4. Work-Life Balance Is Essential to Longevity
   - **Determining what balance means:** to you personally and working to attain it. Prioritizing physical, mental, and emotional health as essential elements of balance is what is meant by "health and well-being."

- **Preventing Burnout:** Spotting the warning symptoms of burnout and proactively preventing it.

5. Lifelong Learning Strategies

- **Setting Learning Goals:** Determining precise targets for the improvement of abilities and knowledge.
- **Dedicated Time:** Setting aside time in daily or weekly schedules only for educational pursuits.
- **Experimentation:** Examining a range of topics to extend horizons and inspire creative thinking.

5. Techniques for Finding Work-Life Balance

- **Time Management:** Setting limits, prioritizing tasks, and efficiently managing time.
- **Delegation:** Assigning work to team members or contracting out to keep attention on high-impact activities.
- **Disconnecting:** Setting aside "off" times and appreciating time spent on activities unrelated to work.

6. Synergy between Balance and Learning

- **Balanced Learning:** Seeking out learning options that mesh with one's personal preferences and support professional obligations.
- **Innovative Mindset:** Fostering creativity and imaginative problem-solving by bringing fresh information and views to the workplace.

- **Learning from Balance:** Recognizing and applying lessons in time management, flexibility, and stress management.

7. Navigating Difficulties

- **Overcommitment:** Striking a balance between the need to study and the reality of having little time and money.
- **Integration:** Finding approaches to effortlessly incorporate educational activities into everyday routines.

6. Setting an Example

- **Entrepreneurial Culture:** Establishing a work-life balance-supportive business culture that fosters learning.
- **Inspiring Teams:** Motivating team members to prioritize their well-being and embrace lifelong learning.

7. The Realization of Harmony and Growth

- **Long-Term Growth:** Understanding that continuing education fosters not just professional but also personal development.
- **Holistic Fulfillment:** Realizing that genuine success includes both career success and personal fulfillment.

The journey of ongoing discovery and equilibrium is discussed in conclusion.

Achieving work-life balance and lifelong learning are related goals that support one another rather than being separate goals. A constant inquiry of broadening perspectives and fostering wellbeing is navigating the world of entrepreneurship. Prioritizing these two pillars helps entrepreneurs create a symbiotic connection that drives them not only toward short-term success but also toward a satisfying, sustainable, and long-lasting journey. An entrepreneur's voyage is woven from the desire of harmony and knowledge, and it is one that is characterized by development, invention, and the unyielding pursuit of a balanced and fulfilling existence.

CHAPTER 9

FUTURE-PROOFING YOUR ENTERPRISE

Strategies for Ensuring Longevity in a Changing Business Environment, Businesses can no longer depend on previous triumphs to secure their future in an age of quick technical breakthroughs, changing customer habits, and unexpected global events. Businesses that proactively adapt, change, and get ready for the uncertainty of tomorrow are the ones that endure. The goal of future-proofing is to thrive in a world that is always changing, not merely to survive. This thorough book explains the idea of future-proofing your business and outlines techniques to guarantee its tenacity and durability.

1. The Need for Forward-Looking Thoughts

Realizing that being stagnant is not an option in the changing world of business. The terrain of tomorrow won't look the same as it does now, thus planning is essential.

2. Accepting technological progress

- **Continuous Tech Education:** Keeping abreast of new developments and comprehending the repercussions.
- **Digital Transformation:** Using digital tools, platforms, and techniques to improve customer experience and simplify operations.

- **Investing in R&D:** Allocating funds for research and development to maintain a position at the forefront of innovation.

3. Business Model Flexibility

   - **Pivot Readiness:** The ability to modify the company model in response to changes in the market or new opportunities.
   - **Scalable Structures:** Creating organizational structures and workflows that may change in response to demand and environmental factors.

4. Increasing the Number of Income Streams

   - **Multiple Income Avenues:** Investigating other goods, services, or markets to lessen dependence on a single income stream.
   - **Passive Income Opportunities:** Creating revenue streams from investments or digital goods that need little continuing work.

5. Building an Organizational Culture That Is Resistant to Change

   - **Adaptive Mindset:** Promoting a culture whereby change is welcomed and staff members are capable of navigating changes.
   - **Continuous Learning:** Motivating staff to upgrade, retool, and broaden their expertise.

6. Making investments in sustainable methods

- **Green Operations:** Using environmentally friendly procedures and goods to satisfy rising customer demand for sustainability.
- **Ethical Business Practices:** Adopting ethical and transparent business practices to foster long-term loyalty and trust.

7. Participating with a Global Mindset

- **Diverse Market Exploration:** Using worldwide markets to disperse risk and seize chances for global development.
- **Cultural Sensitivity:** Appreciating and comprehending various cultural customs and standards in commercial operations.

8 Proactive risk management is number eight.

- **Scenario Planning:** Anticipating probable obstacles or snags and coming up with solutions.
- **Regular Audits:** Periodic reviews and updates of company operations, risk management procedures, and business strategy.

9.Customer-Centric Evolution

- **input Loops:** Regular consumer input collection to improve experiences and services.

- **Anticipating demands:** Adapting to suit changing customer demands and preferences while staying ahead of trends.
8. Leadership Development and Succession Planning
- **Training Future Leaders:** Finding and developing prospective leaders within the company to ensure a seamless transfer.
- **Clear Succession Protocols:** Creating guidelines for executive succession to guarantee company continuity.

The Ongoing Effort of Future-Proofing, Conclusion

Future-proofing requires ongoing work rather than a one-time project. It combines expectation, planning, and adaptability. Businesses may not only survive the winds of change but also harness them by taking a proactive stance and being open to change. In the end, businesses that are aware of the transience of the present and actively plan for the future will prosper. In the constantly changing sands of the commercial environment, they will be the ones to etch pathways of innovation, toughness, and long-lasting success.

Ensuring relevance in a dynamic market

Businesses can no longer depend on previous triumphs to secure their future in an age of quick technical breakthroughs, changing customer habits, and unexpected global events. Businesses that proactively adapt, change, and get ready for the uncertainty of tomorrow are the ones that endure. The goal of future-proofing is to thrive in a world that is always changing, not merely to survive. This thorough book explains the idea of future-proofing your business and outlines techniques to guarantee its tenacity and durability.

1. Introduction: The Need for Forward-Looking Thoughts

Realizing that being stagnant is not an option in the changing world of business. The terrain of tomorrow won't look the same as it does now, thus planning is essential.

2. Accepting technological progress

- **Continuous Tech Education:** Keeping abreast of new developments and comprehending the repercussions.
- **Digital Transformation:** Using digital tools, platforms, and techniques to improve customer experience and simplify operations.
- **Investing in R&D:** Allocating funds for research and development to maintain a position at the forefront of innovation.

3. Business Model Flexibility

- **Pivot Readiness:** The ability to modify the company model in response to changes in the market or new opportunities.
- **Scalable Structures:** Creating organizational structures and workflows that may change in response to demand and environmental factors.

4. Increasing the Number of Income Streams

- **Multiple Income Avenues:** Investigating other goods, services, or markets to lessen dependence on a single income stream.
- **Passive Income Opportunities:** Creating revenue streams from investments or digital goods that need little continuing work.

Building an Organizational Culture That Is Resistant to Change

- **Adaptive Mindset**: Promoting a culture whereby change is welcomed and staff members are capable of navigating changes.
- **Continuous Learning:** Motivating staff to upgrade, retool, and broaden their expertise.
6. Making investments in sustainable methods
- **Green Operations:** Using environmentally friendly procedures and goods to satisfy rising customer demand for sustainability.
- **Ethical Business Practices:** Adopting ethical and transparent business practices to foster long-term loyalty and trust.

7 Participating with a Global Mindset

- **Diverse Market Exploration:** Using worldwide markets to disperse risk and seize chances for global development.

- **Cultural Sensitivity:** Appreciating and comprehending various cultural customs and standards in commercial operations.

8. Proactive risk management

    - **Scenario Planning:** Anticipating probable obstacles or snags and coming up with solutions.
    - **Regular Audits:** Periodic reviews and updates of company operations, risk management procedures, and business strategy.

9. Customer-Centric Evolution

    - **input Loops:** Regular consumer input collection to improve experiences and services.
    - **Anticipating demands:** Adapting to suit changing customer demands and preferences while staying ahead of trends.
    9. Leadership Development and Succession Planning
    - **Training Future Leaders:** Finding and developing prospective leaders within the company to ensure a seamless transfer.
    - **Clear Succession Protocols:** Creating guidelines for executive succession to guarantee company continuity.

The Ongoing Effort of Future-Proofing, Conclusion

Future-proofing requires ongoing work rather than a one-time project. It combines expectation, planning, and adaptability. Businesses may not only survive the winds of change but also harness them by taking a proactive stance and being open to change. In the end, businesses that are aware of the transience of the present and actively plan for the future will prosper. In the constantly changing sands of the commercial environment, they will be the ones to etch pathways of innovation, toughness, and long-lasting success.

Strategies for Business Evolution and Succession Planning

Managing the Enterprise Toward Sustainable Growth and Seamless Transitions: Strategies for Business Evolution and Succession Planning. The corporate world is always moving. An organization must not only adapt to the changing environment but also plan for future leadership changes if it is to endure. The processes of business evolution and succession planning work together to guarantee a company's long-term success and the maintenance of its heritage. This investigation goes deeply into strategic methods for promoting organizational transformation and laying the groundwork for orderly succession.

1. Introduction: The Two Foundations for Long-Term Success

Every successful business must adapt to today's circumstances and make sure that a succession plan is in place for continuity and longevity.

2. Business Evolution: Managing Change, Second Edition

- **Market Analysis:** Consistently evaluate consumer trends, market trends, and competitive environments to guide strategic choices.
- **Innovative Culture:** Encourage workers to submit fresh ideas and solutions by cultivating a creative atmosphere.
- **Diversification:** To reduce risks and access new income sources, expand product lines, penetrate new markets, or provide more services.
- **Digital Transformation:** Use digital technologies, platforms, and techniques to modernize corporate operations, assuring efficiency and bettering consumer experiences.
- **Sustainable Practices:** Include environmentally friendly procedures and social responsibility programs to future-proof the brand and fit with contemporary customer ideals.

3. Setting the Stage for Succession

- **Early Initiatives:** Succession planning shouldn't be something that is done at the last minute; rather, it should be included into the company's strategic strategy from the beginning.
- **Identifying Potential Leaders:** Look for individuals who would become good leaders and fit the company's mission inside the organization.

- **External Recruitment:** External recruiting sometimes offers a new viewpoint. When necessary, think about looking outside the company for prospective successors.

4. Seamless Succession Strategies

- **Mentorship Programs:** Create mentoring programs where existing leaders develop future leaders by sharing crucial information and ideas.
- **Leadership Training:** Make an investment in training courses that emphasize decision-making, crisis management, and leadership abilities.
- **Trial Periods:** Prior to the actual transfer, possible successors may participate in trial periods during which they assume leadership responsibilities in more limited contexts or initiatives.

5. preserving business continuity.

- **Documented Strategies:** Ascertain that operational blueprints, firm values, mission statements, and strategic plans are accessible and well-documented.
- **Stakeholder Communication:** Keep workers, investors, and partners informed about succession plans and changes by engaging with them often.

Implement channels for feedback throughout the transition so that any required modifications may be made in light of the opinions of various stakeholders.

6. Legal and Financial Considerations for Succession

- **Legal Documentation:** Ascertain that any legal paperwork, such as trusts, buy-sell agreements, and wills, are in place and current.
- **Financial Planning:** Consult with financial professionals to determine the transition's effects, taking into account things like taxes, share transfers, and company values.
- **Insurance Mechanisms:** To reduce financial risks during the transfer, look at insurance solutions like key person insurance.

7. Accepting Changing Roles

- **Advisory Positions:** Retiring executives may take up advisory positions where they can provide advice without being engaged in day-to-day activities.
- **Phased Retirement:** To avoid jarring transitions, leaders might progressively scale down their responsibilities.

8. Maintaining Cultural Continuity,

- **Shared Vision:** During the transition, reiterate the company's vision, purpose, and values to maintain cultural consistency.
- **Team Engagement:** During the succession process, include teams, address their issues, and make sure they feel appreciated and vital to the future of the business.

9. Evaluation and Recommendations

- **Regular evaluations:** Following the transition, schedule frequent evaluations to gauge the success of the

changeover and make any required modifications in response to input.
- **Open Channels:** Maintain open lines of contact for staff members and other stakeholders to express suggestions and grievances.

10. Conclusion: Succession and Evolution as Ongoing Efforts

- Planning for succession and business evolution are ongoing activities that need for foresight, readiness, and agility. While evolution:

makes sure a business stays relevant and competitive, succession planning protects its history and guarantees its survival. Together, they provide a comprehensive plan that promotes long-term success, steady development, and smooth leadership changes. Enterprises must adapt as the business environment does by always predicting the next turn and being ready for the road ahead.

CONCLUSION

Making a Long-Lasting Entrepreneurial Legacy, Conclusion

Entrepreneurship is about producing something transcendent, leaving an unmistakable impact that resonates long after one's active engagement fades. It is much more than just the quest of wealth. The creation of a long-lasting entrepreneurial legacy is a complex process that combines vision, values, and influence. Let's explore in depth the subtleties of creating a legacy that not only endures but also serves as a source of inspiration for coming generations as we get to the end of our research.

1. The Quintessence of Legacy, first

Short-term accomplishments or financial success alone do not define a legacy. It concerns the long-lasting change one makes, the standards established, the ideals kept, and the tales that will be passed down through the ages. An entrepreneur's journey culminates in this, which is a reflection of their goals, dedication, and contributions.

2. Leadership with Vision

- **Foresight and Ambition:** Trailblazing business people see possibilities and needs long before others do. Their aspirations go beyond just themselves and often include community, industry, or even world improvement.
- **Embodying fundamental Values:** A solid ethical foundation that forms the legacy is established by consistently supporting and promoting fundamental values, both individually and within the company.

3. Significant Innovations

Legacy-bearing Entrepreneurs often launch game-changing inventions that reshape sectors, influence consumer behavior, and establish new benchmarks.

- **Sustainable Solutions:** Entrepreneurs with a legacy mentality often look for solutions that solve long-term problems, such as social problems and environmental problems, in addition to short-term advantages.
- **Trailblazing:** Legacy is often created by people who are ready to go where no one else has gone before, offering goods, services, or methodologies that spark significant change.

4. Developing future leaders

The leaders that an entrepreneur mentors and develops are a genuine monument to their legacy. They maintain the endurance of their legacy through fostering innovation, imparting information, and instilling ideals.

- **Mentor-ship Programs:** Actively participating in mentoring, providing advice, exchanging experiences, and giving insightful criticism to rising leaders.
- **Promoting inclusion:** Promoting diversity and inclusion, making sure that many viewpoints and voices influence how the organization develops.

5. Community involvement and charitable giving

An entrepreneur's involvement in their society and charitable work is closely related to their legacy.

- **Social Initiatives:** Creating organizations or doing projects that benefit the neighborhood, deal with urgent problems, or promote well-being, health, and education.
- **Empowering Others:** An entrepreneur's influence is boosted by providing possibilities for others, whether via employment, joint ventures, or charitable endeavors.

6 Adapting and Evolving

The corporate environment is dynamic. Entrepreneurs that succeed in the long run are those who are willing to change, grow, and reinvent themselves in order to keep their businesses current.

- **Continuous Learning:** Adopting a lifetime learning philosophy, keeping up with changes in the business, and persistently seeking out information.
- **Embracing Change:** Legacy-minded business owners utilize change rather than fighting it because they view it as an opportunity for expansion and reinvention.

7. Tenacity and perseverance

Challenges often give rise to legacies. The story of an entrepreneur's path and legacy is shaped by the endurance and resilience shown in the face of challenges, disappointments, and failures.

- **Learning from Failures**: View setbacks as stepping stones, gather knowledge, and improve tactics rather than letting them discourage you.
- **Enduring Spirit:** Demonstrating steadfast dedication, especially under trying circumstances, inspiring trust and awe in peers, staff, and stakeholders.

8. Maintaining Continuity

A lasting legacy requires consistency. The development of sustainable company models, strategic road-maps, and succession planning are crucial.

- **Future-Proofing:** Putting plans into place to make sure the company is robust and relevant in a competitive market.

- **Shared goal:** Including all relevant parties, from partners to workers, and ensuring that they share the entrepreneur's goal and are motivated to see it through.

9. Final Thoughts

It takes enormous effort to create an enduring entrepreneurial legacy, which is characterized by vision, tenacity, invention, and influence. It involves building something bigger than oneself, having an impact on several businesses, changing society, and motivating future generations. Entrepreneurs build not just their legacy but also the fundamental foundation of the entrepreneurial ecosystem as they set out on this significant journey. In order to ensure that their legacy endures, not just in terms of their material accomplishments but also in the inspiration they provide, the standards they establish, and the change they bring in, their undertakings, values, and tales become the beacons for those who come after them.

10. Legacy's Ethical Foundations

A strong ethical basis is the cornerstone of a lasting legacy, in addition to monetary success and industry recognition. A legacy of respect and admiration is left behind by business people who place a high priority on honesty, ethics, and openness.

- **company Ethics:** Upholding moral integrity in all company contacts, from supplier negotiations to customer relations, and making sure it isn't sacrificed for immediate profits.

- **Accountability:** Accepting accountability for actions, whether positive and negative, builds trust and creates a reputation for dependability and trustworthiness.

11. The Influence of Relationships

Business is primarily about connections, not simply transactions. An entrepreneurial legacy gains depth through appreciating and nurturing these relationships, whether they be with partners, customers, workers, or other stakeholders.

- **People-First Approach:** Treating everyone with respect and dignity while appreciating the value of each person's contribution to the company's success.
- **Collaborative Success:** Appreciating cooperation and partnerships and realizing that group efforts often produce better results than solo ones.

12. Environmental Stewardship

Environmental issues are of utmost importance in the modern society. Entrepreneurs that actively address these problems and adopt sustainable methods not only improve the condition of the earth, but also create a legacy that is admired for its innovative spirit.

- **Eco-Friendly Initiatives:** Putting into effect methods that lessen waste, save resources, and have a minimal negative impact on the environment.

- **Sustainable Growth:** Making sure that corporate development doesn't harm the environment by balancing growth with ecological responsibility.

13. The Effects of Knowledge Sharing

One of the most durable methods to establish one's legacy is via imparting information. The entrepreneurial community as a whole expands thanks to entrepreneurs who share their knowledge, skills, and ideas.

- **Educational Initiatives:** Creating courses, seminars, or even institutions that encourage education and skill development.
- **Writing and Speaking:** Writing books, articles, or giving speeches to reach a wider audience.

14. Promoting an Innovative Culture

In order to leave a lasting legacy, one must first establish the foundation for future possibilities. The business will continue to develop if a culture that values innovation is fostered.

- **Open Platforms:** Establishing areas where staff members of all ranks may present ideas to prevent the stifling of creativity.
- **Rewarding Creativity:** Setting up procedures to acknowledge and honor original thoughts, demonstrating the importance of original thought to the company.

15. Final Reflections

Vision, principles, partnerships, ideas, moral judgments, and innumerable instances of tenacity and resiliency are just a few of the many components that make up an entrepreneurial legacy. Building such a legacy is an ongoing journey rather than a destination or milestone. Each choice, no matter how significant, contributes a piece to this complex jigsaw. Entrepreneurs' long legacies serve as testaments to the depth of their journey, the difficulties they overcame, and the good effect they have had on the world. These legacies stand out in the annals of business history, leading and motivating future generations.